The "Other"
State Department

/

The "Other" State Department

The United States Mission
to the United Nations—
Its Role in the
Making of Foreign Policy

ARNOLD BEICHMAN

FOREWORD BY LELAND M. GOODRICH,
JAMES T. SHOTWELL PROFESSOR OF
INTERNATIONAL RELATIONS,
COLUMBIA UNIVERSITY

Basic Books, Inc., Publishers
NEW YORK / LONDON

To Carroll Aikins Beichman

Foreword

LELAND M. GOODRICH
*James T. Shotwell Professor of International Relations,
Columbia University*

During the period of the League of Nations many members adopted the practice of establishing permanent delegations in Geneva which served as diplomatic missions to the Organization. Even the United States, though not a member, accorded its consulate in Geneva the status of a permanent mission, the function of which was to serve as a reporting agency and as a channel of communications between Washington and the League. This practice of establishing permanent missions was not initially welcomed by the League Secretariat, which at an early stage expressed a preference for dealing directly with each member government through a special office of League affairs which it hoped each member would establish in its foreign office. Sir Eric Drummond and his advisers at first feared that the establishment of permanent delegations would interpose an unnecessary obstacle between the Organization and member states and consequently cause the Organization to lose touch with capitals where the decisions of member governments were made. The Swiss Government also was not particularly happy to have a second diplomatic corps on its territory, in addition to that at Bern, with claims to special privileges and immunities. The advantages of permanent delegations came to be recognized, however, and the institution became an accepted part of the Geneva scene though never achieving the significant role in League affairs that its successor has achieved in the work of the United Nations.

With the establishment of the United Nations and the decision to locate its headquarters in New York, the establishment of permanent missions by members of the Organization became a common practice. For members of the Security Council, it was in a sense a legal obligation to maintain such missions since the Council was required by the Charter to be so organized as to be able to function continuously. For other members it became an equally compelling necessity because of the scope of the Organization's activities, the importance of being continuously informed about them, and the need to be prepared for effective participation in meetings. The advantages indeed were so numerous and obvious as hardly to need enumeration here. For those members who might be thought least able to afford permanent missions the advantages were particularly compelling since, with other members generally following the practice, a mission at United Nations headquarters made possible a range of contacts with other countries that could otherwise be achieved only through a large and costly number of individual diplomatic missions maintained at national capitals. While permanent missions at the United Nations did not eliminate the need of such individual country missions it substantially reduced the number that were necessary. But of course the chief advantage of permanent missions lay in providing an effective channel of communication with the Organization and a base for organizing and carrying out effective participation in meetings of the General Assembly and other organs in New York.

While the permanent mission takes on the aspect and has many of the functions of a diplomatic mission to another state, the fact of its being accredited to an international organization gives it a special character and imposes special responsibilities. Though the permanent representative has the responsibility to represent his government in various discussions, negotiations, and meetings held under United Nations auspices, he must also keep his government informed about what is transpiring within the Organization and thereby provide information essential to his government in determining policies to be followed in a wide variety of matters. The fact that he very often is engaged in discussions or negotiations where the reactions of many parties need to be taken into account, where quick tactical decisions have to be made based on estimates of situations that are rapidly changing and that

he is in the best position to make, and where the final
result may have important political and psychological
consequences places upon the permanent representative, as
the man on the spot, a particularly heavy responsibility.
It suggests that the effective participation of his country
in the work of the Organization may require that he
should have a greater freedom of action and a larger
measure of participation in the formation of the policy
he is expected to carry out than is the case with the
normal diplomatic representative.

There has been very little serious exploration by scholars
or other informed persons of what the role of the permanent representative vis-à-vis his government is in actual
practice. The assumption that it is similar to that of the
head of a diplomatic mission in a foreign country to his
government certainly cannot be accepted without question. It is, of course, a very difficult subject to investigate
because the evidence is elusive and is not to be found in
documentary materials to any great extent. Even the testi-
mony of participants may not be too fully relied upon,
considering their personal involvement. Relations between
the interested parties may be of such a confidential nature
and so closely related to highly sensitive matters that
there is an unwillingness on the part of those directly involved to divulge details. In time, with the opening of
confidential files to the scrutiny of scholars, a more com-
plete story may be told. On the other hand, the increasing
reliance on telephonic and oral communication in recent

years, especially in relations between the United States Permanent Mission and Washington policy-makers, may reduce the value of the documentary record when available and suggests the desirability of probing the experience of living participants to the extent they are prepared to talk.

Arnold Beichman has performed a real service in his effort to clarify the relationship of the United States Permanent Mission and, more particularly, the Permanent Representative to the policy-makers in Washington. His personal contacts with the principal actors and his close relation to events at the United Nations have made it possible for him to write with authority. He has brought to his task the training of a scholar and the experience of a skilled journalist, and while he has not said the last word on the subject he has given us a substantial introduction to it. He has also emphasized the desirability of similar inquiries into the relation of other permanent missions to other governments.

He is primarily concerned in this book with the relation of the permanent mission to the national government—its role in the making of the policy of the member government. There is another angle that is greatly in need of detailed investigation—the relation of the mission to the Secretariat. A former member of the Secretariat whose wisdom I greatly respected—William M. Jordan—used to speak of the permanent missions as being partly in the Secretariat. This is an angle that Beichman recognizes in

Foreword

his book and to some extent explores. I judge his view to be that the United States Permanent Mission participates in the making of United States policy by interpreting and defending the United States commitment to and interest in the United Nations. If one were writing the kind of book that Jordan had in mind, the emphasis would be on the role of the Permanent Mission in conveying to the Secretary-General and his staff the particular points of view and interests of the United States as a member of the Organization and thereby contributing to the discharge of the Secretary-General's responsibilities for promoting international harmony and cooperation. These two functions and responsibilities are equally important to the success of the United Nations and the effectiveness of member participation in it.

New York
1968

Preface

This is a study of the relationship between the Department of State and the United States Mission to the United Nations (USUN) during the period 1946–1968. Inevitably it is also a study of the men who, as ambassadors, have headed the USUN. Since little has been written about USUN, either as history or as part of the American governmental process (that is, the informal process rather than the formal structure), this study traverses unknown ground. To eliminate misunderstanding I want to state here what the study is not and, as they say in the House of Commons, declare my interest.

First, then, I am an admirer of former Ambassador Goldberg, who served for almost three years as USUN Chief. Unhappily, I am not his confidant although he was good enough to grant me several interviews during the course of my researches. This book does not claim to be the inside story of what goes on in the Ambassador's office or at his residence.

Second, this study obviously could not deal with USUN under Ambassador George Ball, who was to succeed Goldberg in June 1968.

Third, the study is not about the UN, except peripherally.

Fourth, I am not suggesting that USUN is really the State Department or that the latter is an overlord of which USUN is a feudatory. I am calling it the "other" State Department because there does not seem to be any category into which USUN easily fits. It is surely not an embassy in the ordinary sense, nor does it resemble one of the many independent administrative agencies within the Federal establishment. Nor is it analogous to the United States missions to other international bodies, like NATO or OAS. Nor is it a geographical or regional bureau within the State Department. Nor is there any precedent for USUN since the United States was not a member of the League of Nations and thus did not develop the traditions for a civil service assigned to international organizations.

Fifth, I am not suggesting that the USUN Chief is the Secretary of State, the President, or the UN Secretary-General. His title is a useful clue to what he does but not much more than that. It is no accident that the five men who have headed USUN since its establishment—Senators Austin and Lodge, Adlai Stevenson, Arthur J. Goldberg, and George Ball—have been prominent figures who so far as the United States Foreign Service is concerned were "outsiders," men of strong opinions and large constituencies.[1] From the State Department bureaucratic standpoint, such men can be characterized as trouble-makers, boat-rockers, nonconformists.

The purpose of this book is to examine the growth of an institution called USUN as a subsystem within the American foreign policy subsystem on the one hand and as a subsystem within the larger UN subsystem on the other, a state of affairs with schizoid implications for USUN.[2] One can argue, as I do, that USUN has achieved an influence in the formulation of foreign policy suggesting autonomy, an influence which no other diplomatic mission in the government would be allowed to claim.[3] I shall attempt to test several propositions dealing with USUN's attributes, roles, relationships, and resources. (For example, what does it mean to USUN's aspirations for superordination when it is headed by men who, with one exception, can rightfully claim a personal relationship with the President?) I have found instances where USUN exercised "home-rule" prerogatives, entirely of its own making, refusing to submit to a State Department policy line unpalatable to the USUN Chief or to officials within the department itself but outside USUN. At the very least, USUN has had to coexist with the State Department in what Wallace S. Sayre has described in another context as "a system of shared powers and functions." Has USUN reached a certain organizational stability accompanied by the persistence, over twenty years, of certain definable characteristics, and recurrences of the same kinds of conflicts between the Department and USUN?

In pursuing my researches, I began to understand what Herbert Feis meant by his phrase "the shackled historian" and by his statement that "bountiful bibliography is not the equivalent of bountiful knowledge."[4] By the time I had completed my preliminary findings and interviews, I was tempted to consider myself the "shackled" political scientist *manqué*. Primary sources about USUN are few. Open sources tend to be misleading and self-validating.[5] They respect the first half of C. P. Scott's famous dictum, "Comment is free but facts are sacred," but care little for the second half. Some interviewees were unwilling to be quoted by name or even to be described by present or onetime government roles.

Why, then, should one undertake a journey into contemporary history via political science technology? Because USUN has been involved in some major episodes in American foreign policy decision-making; because it is an integral part of a world institution with enormous moral meaning; because several outstanding Americans have found the post of USUN Chief prestigious enough to satisfy ambition and idealism at the same time; and because I have been fortunate enough to find some unpublished material for case studies bearing upon the making of foreign policy within a UN context. Not everything I cite will be footnoted. Such is the price a researcher must pay when he involves himself in contemporary history. Journalists easily become accustomed to citing "informed sources," "usually reliable quarters," "diplomatic informants." Often these phrases confirm a fidelity to ritual if not necessarily to accuracy. The academic commitment bars such anonymous sources as a substitute for scholarly research except in rare cases. This work, I hope, will be one of those rare cases.[6]

My gratitude for their valuable criticisms goes to Professor Wallace S. Sayre of Columbia University whose ideas and lectures influenced me greatly and to Professor Leland M. Goodrich, also of Columbia, for starting me on these researches. Among UN journalists I must thank five men who may not know it but whose knowledge I have tapped over the years: Louis B. Fleming, Los Angeles *Times-Mirror*; Earl Foell, *Christian Science Monitor*; Richard C. Hottelet, Columbia Broadcasting System; Drew Middleton, *The New York Times*; and Paul Ward, Baltimore *Sun*. Irving Brown, for many years UN representative for the International Confederation of Free Trade Unions, was exceedingly helpful. A number of State Department and USUN officers, past and present, have understandably asked that their names be omitted from the credits. One former USUN official has my heartfelt gratitude, my friend, Ernest A. Gross, who was generous with his time and suggestions. Interviews with Robert D. Murphy and Andrew Cordier afforded me indispensable insights into the US–USUN–UN system. For what I have written, I alone am responsible.

ARNOLD BEICHMAN

New York
June 1968

Notes

1. Two other USUN Chiefs were ad interim and are referred to further on. One deputy USUN Chief, Ernest A. Gross, was so frequently in charge of the Mission because of the protracted illness of his superior, Senator Austin, that he could easily rank as a de facto USUN Chief.

2. A subsystem is defined as "an element or functional component of a larger system which fulfills the conditions of a system in itself but which also plays a specialized role in the operation of the larger system." (Oran R. Young, "A Survey of General Systems Theory," in *General Systems*, IX [1964], p. 69.) For another definition, see Chapter 7, note 26.

3. ". . . Influence is a *relation among actors* in which one actor induces other actors to act in some way they would not otherwise act." (Robert A. Dahl, *Modern Political Analysis* [Englewood Cliffs, N.J.: Prentice-Hall, 1963], p. 40.) "In the American system each policy area has a high degree of autonomy. American government, Ernest Griffith has said, is 'government by whirlpools.'" (Zbigniew Brzezinski and Samuel P. Huntington, *USA/USSR* [New York: Viking Press paperback, 1965], p. 226.)

4. Herbert Feis, "The Shackled Historian," *Foreign Affairs*, XLV, No. 2 (January 1967), 331–343.

5. "Clearly the standard methods of attitude measurement—the personal interview, the questionnaire, or direct observation of decisionmakers in action—can rarely be used by the social scientist who seeks to study human behavior at the international level." (Robert C. North, Ole R. Holsti, Richard A. Brody, *Perception and Action in the Study of*

International Relations: The 1914 Crisis, Quoted by David C. Schwartz, "Decision Theories and Crisis Behavior," *Orbis,* XI, No. 2 [Summer 1967], 467.)

6. "Identifying precisely the sources of policy is a difficult task for the scholar in almost any political system." (Brzezinski and Huntington, *op. cit.,* p. 203.)

Contents

Contents

The "Other"
State Department

1 / Introduction

Lincoln Bloomfield has written:

Students of international organization, like students of domestic government, usually focus their attention on problems of formal organizational structure and arrangements and quite often neglect the sub-stratum of informal operations and relationships. The study of public administration, in its quest for greater depth of perception, has in recent years gained rich insights through analysis of the informal and human aspects of policy-making. But international organization, still a parvenu from the American standpoint, has scarcely felt the scalpel of this particular form of dissection.[1]

Although this statement is not so applicable today as when it was made in 1958, it is still true that little has been reported about the actual operations of USUN, its living system, its subsystem, its assorted roles, its boundaries. Let me first define these analytic phrases. "The living system represents how things are, not merely how they are supposed to be," writes Chris Argyris.[2] David Easton has suggested that subsystems abstract "from the

3

whole social system some variables which seem to cohere more closely than others . . . and to look upon them as a subsystem which can be profitably examined, temporarily, apart from the whole social system."[3] And Robert Dahl points out that one system can be an element or a subsystem within another and that something can be a subsystem in two or more different systems that overlap in part.[4]

Were the USUN regarded as an independent executive agency, on the style of the Civil Aeronautics Administration or the Civil Service Commission or the Army Corps of Engineers, it would by now probably have received the attention it merits. It would have been examined from the standpoint of its relation to the Presidency, Congress, the lobbyists or the special-interest groups, the press, the congressional committees and their staffs, and other diplomatic missions. Is the United States Chief of Mission to the UN also the UN Ambassador to the United States? And if he is, what would this dual role mean? Ambassador Arthur J. Goldberg declared a few months after accepting the appointment:

> I consider the role of the United States representative to the United Nations to be a dual one. He, of course, first represents the President of our government at the UN; but, second, he also represents the UN to the American people.[5]

It may be suggested that it is not unusual for an ambassador to become so enamored of the host country that he sometimes acts in an ambivalent fashion. Howard P.

4

Jones, the long-time envoy to Indonesia, was thus affected, as was Joseph E. Davies in Stalin's Soviet Union. Chester Bowles in India has been criticized as being over-indulgent toward the Indian government and peoples. Probably one of the most extraordinary periods in modern American diplomacy was the two years and nine months of Joseph P. Kennedy's ambassadorship to the United Kingdom. Kennedy was accused of being sympathetic to the Cliveden set and to Hitler and of being disloyal to President Roosevelt. He was even reprimanded in a personal letter by President Roosevelt for an indiscreet newspaper interview. In fact, a gibe at the time attributed to Mrs. Harold Ickes had it that "Neville Chamberlain has decided to increase his Cabinet so he can give Joe Kennedy a place in it."[6] One can mention other American envoys who have fallen in love with their assignments, but the reasons for such bigamous cravings may be a function of some ambassadorial personal idiosyncrasy, like a passion for Persian culture or some rabid form of Francophilia. Certainly no American diplomat would dream of suggesting a dualism in the manner of Justice Goldberg's rhetoric. The fact that such a statement as his can be made without causing a ripple may reflect, first, the depth of the American commitment, official and private, to the UN; second, what a unique position the USUN chief representative holds in the national and international community.

In one of the Hammarskjöld lectures, Sir Muhammad

The "Other" State Department

Zafrulla Khan demonstrated that the sense of dualism pervades not only American delegates to the UN but also delegates of other countries:

> As one delegate put it upon leaving the United Nations: Here as Ambassador I wore two hats: one as the representative of my country, expressing and championing its views as necessary in matters of direct concern to it, but also I valued highly the opportunity of wearing the second hat, which was made possible by the ratification by my country of the Charter of the UN, placing it under obligations of great importance.[7]

This "political dualism," I would suggest, gives rise to a basic dualism in responsibility because the foundation of the USUN is both the United States Constitution and the UN Charter, the latter a treaty ratified by the Senate. This dualism may well create conflicts within the State Department such as have been attributed to officials in international secretariats.[8]

There seems to be little question, as I hope to show, that USUN has become a major factor in the decision-making process of American foreign policy. It might even be argued and demonstrated that USUN has made (or unmade) policy or pressed a point of view which neither the State Department nor even the White House staff had originally shared. In fact, President Kennedy is said to have recognized this state of affairs by referring to USUN as "my other State Department in New York."[9] Few developments and proposals by Washington policymakers become final without some formal or informal check with USUN.

It would, of course, be emphasizing the obvious to say that the USUN is far more than an embassy and that the Chief of Mission enjoys far greater status than even his exalted diplomatic title might imply.[10] I hope to explore the role of Mission Chief in some detail as well as the role of the USUN itself in different relationships within the government, public opinion and press media, UN delegations, and some special-interest groups.[11] I shall hope to show (though by no means conclusively) that USUN has almost as many involvements in the course of its operations as does the State Department.[12] Among the reasons for this is that the USUN has a more direct relationship with various publics than the Department.[13] Like the UN, it has built up a large constituency and thus has become a direct participant, a partner, *secundus inter pares* in foreign policy formulation, within the State Department.

These statements should be testable in some manner. Yet the testing could not be conclusive. For example, take the question of USUN boundary within the State Department. A boundary is defined as something which "can be assigned to a political system wherever there exists a sharp decline in the power of the government of the system to influence action."[14] With such a test it is not easy to define the USUN boundary except by case history or by empirical observation, which in itself may be ultimately misleading as either proving too much or proving too little. Or the question of USUN resources arises. A political resource is defined as "a means whereby one person can influence the behavior of other persons [but] control over political resources is unevenly distributed in virtually all societies."[15] All that can be offered here is a form of subjective judgment, based on interviews with individuals involved in the subsystems as well as on more objective data. And even that may be insufficient if one accepts Hobbes's statement that "reputation of power is power."[16] So reputation for autonomy may create autonomy, a form of self-fulfilling prophecy. Can one measure autonomy on a scale—from autonomy (total) to subservivence (total)? Can one measure authority? Can one really know the quality of interpersonal relationship between a Secretary of State and a USUN Chief without access to classified documents and diaries or listening to conversations?

A paradigm of politics has been offered by William H. Riker along these lines. A tells B to do H. A instigates, B responds; B either complies or does not comply. The Authority (upper-case) is A's right of command; the authority (lower-case) consists in the fact that B listens to A. The upper-case Authority puts into order the instigations from lower-case authorities—small a's—and this ordering, says Riker, is the essence of politics. There are lots of lower-case authorities competing to command B. The question of authority revolves around the question as to who will decide among the instigations to which B must react—what A says or what the small a's say.[17]

To apply such a paradigm in the USUN–State Depart-

ment relationship becomes a rather complicated procedure. While A (or State) has the right of command over
B (USUN), there are occasions, as we shall see, where B
has told A to do H or B may have forced A to do H. This
arises from the fact that while we know where A belongs
in the American political system, it is not always evident
where B belongs—to A or to another legitimate actor, C,
the United Nations subsystem. C is not merely just another host country, and B is not merely just another
embassy location. For the American government, the
UN is *sui generis* among international organizations, with
linkages in all directions.

Perhaps the Riker paradigm, with its theory of ordering, affords a useful insight into the State–USUN relationship. If the essence of politics is ordering of instigations, whoever does the ordering or has the final say may
be superordinate or "more equal." Here again we find a
conflict or at least a source of variation. Assuming a
unitary interest, State would like to see one ordering of
instigations of USUN, while UN or UN member nations
would like to see another sequence. USUN may accept
the Department's sequence, but there is frequently a
problem because of the fundamental difference in what
Karl Deutsch has called "the strategy of values" between
State, USUN, and UN. That difference is expressed in
what each Authority would like to see as the ordering of
instigations. Every aspirant to political leadership seeks to
transmute influence into upper-case Authority. In seeking

9

to adapt the Riker paradigm to my purposes, I am mindful of the dangers of reductive paralogisms, but they are unavoidable if we are better to understand the living systems of governmental organizations.

Thus far I have outlined three major propositions which I shall try to test: Does USUN enjoy any special kind of autonomy? What is the special participant role of the USUN Chief in foreign policy decision-making? Does USUN belong to the UN in the sense that no other United States mission ever "belongs" to the host country in which it is located?

From these propositions follow these subpropositions:

1. USUN derives some of its important resources from the historic development of international organizations in the past century within the nation-state system (as a means, say, of achieving national policy objectives). More specifically, USUN gets supplemental strength from the very existence of the UN. No strength necessarily accrues to a United States ambassador in a foreign country because of that country's existence. But precisely because of the UN, USUN and its Chief are enriched—so long as the American government sees in the UN a way of forwarding essential policies.

2. Because the UN has received strong public support from its inception and because of congressional bipartisanship on the UN, USUN has forged valuable alliances with various publics—what has been called "the community of the concerned"[18]—and with Congress itself.

3. Because of its unusual "living system," as distinguished from that of the State Department or other embassies, USUN can afford risks which State cannot. Specifically, the USUN Chief, noncareer-oriented, can take risks which few other State Department officials would.

4. Since the Mission lives within a quasi-parliamentary environment—open debates, annual meetings, committee hearings, budget-making, and, above all, the roll-call vote —it frequently becomes an action-forcing, action-producing agency within the entire United States government, not merely as a branch of the State Department.[19] It is always involved in "crisis" politics such as the Congo, Suez, Article 19, Vietnam, or the Middle East.

5. Because the USUN "belongs" to the UN as well as to the State Department, the Mission becomes a negotiating arm of the UN when it deals with the State Department even while it is a subordinate agency of the Department.

6. The "manifest functions" of the USUN—that is, those intended and recognized by Congress and President in the Dumbarton Oaks–San Francisco era—have been extended with the development of USUN's "latent functions"—those unintended and unrecognized by the laws which originally institutionalized the Mission.

7. From the State Department standpoint, USUN processes may arguably be dysfunctional to American foreign policy because of the multifarious Mission and

ambassadorial roles. For example, an issue which to State may be peripheral to American policy aims may be forced into a central position because of the UN-USUN "partnership" and UN mediatory authority (a UN "latent function") between USUN and State. From a USUN standpoint, its role is not at all dysfunctional because by contributing to UN prestige, influence, and authority it is fulfilling the stated aims of President and Congress while at the same time it is strengthening itself against State Department pressures. Yet one cannot say that the State–USUN bargaining process is a zero-sum game, in which USUN authority maximization is on some one-to-one or other ratio basis with State. It could well be a positive-sum game, this mix of conflict and bargaining—especially if it can increase the positive sum.[20]

8. The Chief of Mission post presents difficulties in political analysis. The overwhelming majority of USUN officials are career officers either in the Foreign Service or Civil Service. With one short-term exception, the Chiefs of Mission came from outside the career foreign service. Is the Chief of Mission a separate actor playing many roles and enjoying star billing, as when he is discussed as a Senatorial or Vice-Presidential candidate or even as the successor to the Secretary of State himself?[21] Adlai Stevenson had power—negative power, perhaps—but little authority within the foreign policy machine. (I shall deal with Stevenson's negative power in Chapter 9 in connection with the Article 19 fight over Soviet arrearages.)

One might argue that the UN existence and status within the United States foreign policy machine means that the USUN must be dealt with as a "foreign power," no matter who the Ambassador is. The USUN Chief can derail foreign policy decisions when he has such manifold resources that he enjoys an immunity from reprisal, and particularly when he is not career-oriented. Is the USUN Chief policy-maker or policy-executor, or both, and in what sequence?

Perhaps one could deal with the USUN Chief in terms of role analysis because of "the conflicting obligations stemming from the actor's simultaneous occupancy of two positions"—U.S. Ambassador to UN and "UN Ambassador to U.S."—even though he is the incumbent of a single position.[22]

9. If it is tenable that "ultimately, the power of government comes to rest in the administrative branch [and] that the President and Congress have only sporadic control over the administrative process,"[23] can we define USUN as the administering arm of American policy at the UN with maximizing opportunities similar to those attendant on other administrative agencies?

In testing these propositions, I shall be mindful of A. J. Ayer's definition of "the mark of a genuine factual proposition [is] that some experiential propositions can be deduced from it in conjunction with certain other premises without being deducible from these other premises alone."[24]

Notes

1. Lincoln Bloomfield, "American Policy Toward the UN—Some Bureaucratic Reflections," *International Organization*, XII (1958), p. 1. In a somewhat different use of the substratum concept, David Lockwood has written that "what may be called the substratum of social action, especially as it conditions interests which are productive of social conflict and instability, tends to be ignored as a general determinant of the dynamics of social systems." (*British Journal of Sociology*, VIII, No. 2 [1956], 210.)

2. U.S. Department of State, Publication No. 8180, Center for International Systems Research, *Some Causes of Organizational Ineffectiveness within the Department of State*. Occasional Papers No. 2, January 1967. Or as Woodrow Wilson wrote: "The leading inquiry in the examination of any system of government must, of course, concern primarily the real depositaries and the essential machinery of power. There is always a centre of power; where in this system is that centre? In whose hands is self-sufficient authority lodged and through what agencies does that authority speak and act?" (*Congressional Government*, 15th ed. [New York: Meridian, 1956], pp. 30–31.)

3. David Easton, *The Political System* (New York: Knopf, 1953), pp. 96–99.

4. Robert A. Dahl, *Modern Political Analysis* (Englewood Cliffs, N.J.: Prentice-Hall, 1963), p. 9.

5. Address before the United Nations Association of the United States, November 11, 1965. Francis T. P. Plimpton, who served as Deputy Representative for USUN under Adlai Stevenson, has written: "In a sense, a U.S. Ambassador to the U.N. is a U.N. Ambassador to the U.S." (Edward P. Doyle [ed.], *As We Knew Adlai: The Stevenson Story* [New York: Harper and Row, 1966], p. 259.)

6. Richard J. Whalen, *The Founding Father: The Story of Joseph P. Kennedy* (New York: Signet, 1966), pp. 210, 219, 231, 244, 250, 258, *et passim*. There is a fine irony of history in the widespread attack at the time on Kennedy that as the United States Ambassador he had supported the Chamberlain-Hitler Munich Pact in 1938. Almost a quarter-century later, Adlai Stevenson was accused by unnamed individuals, obviously with close White House connections, of having wanted, against the wishes of President Kennedy, "a Munich" during the 1962 Cuban missile crisis. I deal with this story, as it affected the

USUN, in Chapter 9. Sir Harold Nicolson has written: "There is always a tendency among diplomatists who have resided for long in foreign countries, and who have perhaps fallen out of contact with their own people and with their own foreign office, to find that their loyalties become a trifle blurred." (*Diplomacy* [New York: Oxford University Press, 1964], p. 65.)

7. Andrew Cordier and Wilder Foote (eds.), *The Quest for Peace* (New York: Columbia University Press, 1965), p. 171. The concept of "political dualism" was expounded by John Locke in "A Letter Concerning Toleration," wherein he maintained that a man's actions are subject to the jurisdiction of "the outward and inward court"—the church and the state, the civil and ecclesiastical authorities. Tocqueville "detects a moral dualism in American character. Coupled with intense concern for private, material welfare is a propensity for periodic moral and religious enthusiasm." (Gabriel A. Almond, *The American People and Foreign Policy* [New York: Praeger, 1960], p. 32.) Despite this dualism, few, if any, other UN missions act with the same independence of their Foreign Offices as does USUN. Generally speaking, when a UN ambassador acts autonomously because of the "two hats" syndrome, it is because his Foreign Office or sovereign is uninterested in the issue involved or in the vote to be taken.

8. "An international secretariat, composed of nationals of a variety of states, has direct contact with an international entity. Do its loyalty mechanisms differ from those of persons who are more indirectly related to international organizations? Practical people, basing opinion on their League of Nations experience, argue (with much agreement among themselves) that international loyalty is not the denationalized loyalty of the man without a country but . . . is the conviction that the highest interests of one's own country are served best by the promotion of security and welfare everywhere. . . . In what way does the type of international organization to which one is associated affect the loyalty problem?" (Harold Guetzkow, *Multiple Loyalties: Theoretical Approach to a Problem in International Organization*, Publication No. 4, Center for Research on World Political Institutions [Princeton: 1955].)

9. I have been unable to track down a source for this phrase, but it was heard among White House staffers and attributed to the President. According to Pierre Salinger's memoir *With Kennedy* (New York: Doubleday, 1966), the White House assigned Arthur Schlesinger, Jr., to be liaison with Adlai Stevenson in addition to the normal State Department relationship with USUN. In any case, whether the quotation is apocryphal or not, the State Department people refer to USUN

as "New York," not in the fashion that they would say "London" or "Paris," but in a tone of voice which indicates they sometimes feel they are dealing with a foreign power. Francis Plimpton (Doyle, *op. cit.*, p. 261), who served as Stevenson's deputy, writes: "A sometimes heard USUN saying is that it's easier to deal with the Soviets than with the [State] Department." Of course, it's nothing new to have "another State Department": Colonel House, Raymond Moley, Harry Hopkins, were *personal* encroachments, however, on the State Department, not institutional. For more on these encroachments, see "Special Diplomatic Agents of the President," *Annals of the American Academy*, CCCVII (September 1956), p. 124.

10. The Chief of Mission's full title reads "Ambassador Extraordinary" (because he represents the person of the President as well as the Government of the United States), and "Plenipotentiary" indicates his full power to negotiate. This is not an uncommon title in the diplomatic establishment. (Department of State Publication No. 6420, Department and Foreign Service Series 60 [January 1957].)

11. James McCamy, *Conduct of the New Diplomacy* (New York: Harper and Row, 1964), pp. 4, 5. The author points out that foreign policy decision-making involves seven actors—(1) communications media; (2) the public as: (*a*) mass public, (*b*) smaller *attentive* public of any issue, (*c*) smaller *expressive* public of any issue, (*d*) electorate; (3) organized interest groups; (4) individuals, business firms, private institutions which influence public stands; (5) Congress through (*a*) committees, (*b*) staff, (*c*) party leaders, (*d*) individual Representatives; (6) the Chief Executive and the Executive establishment; and (7) officials of other nations in Washington or at home. Strangely, McCamy omits the UN and its Secretary-General.

12. In a sense, the USUN Chief is also the United States Ambassador to the other national delegations represented at the UN and presumably he or his subordinates are in some kind of regular contact the year around with other mission chiefs, whether formally or informally.

13. Paul Appleby, *Policy and Administration* (University: University of Alabama Press, 1949), p. 38, describes eight political processes. The seventh includes agencies, like the State Department, as examples of executive agencies whose "activities (are) fairly sharply separated from the general social scene and not fully open to popular pressure. . . . The State Department has little direct contact with citizens and citizens little direct contact association with the Department." Also see, below, Chapter 13, footnote 1.

14. Dahl, *op. cit.*, p. 23.

15. *Ibid.,* p. 15.

16. Thomas Hobbes, *Leviathan* (Chicago: Henry Regnery, 1956), p. 81.

17. William H. Riker, "Review of Bernard de Jouvenel's *The Pure Theory of Politics*" (New Haven: Yale University Press, 1963), in *Journal of Conflict Resolution,* IX, No. 3 (1965), 375–376. In Riker's essay review he says that "in the paradigm 'A tells B to do H'—as political scientists we care nothing about A's or B's motives. Our interest is what A *says* and what B *does*. We need no theory of human nature —it only confuses us, as it does de Jouvenel" (p. 379). I intend to exploit Riker's slighting the interaction of personality in decision-making when I come to the USUN under Ambassador Lodge, Chapter 7.

18. Harland Cleveland, "Crisis Diplomacy," *Foreign Affairs,* XLI, No. 4 (July 1963), 639.

19. For example, American policy on Southwest Africa took a specific turn October 27, 1966, when the USUN backed a resolution declaring the South African mandate at an end. The resolution set up an *ad hoc* committee to report to a special General Assembly session by April 1967 "practical means" for implementing the resolution. This deadline forced action (or inaction) and specific evaluation by other agencies of the government of what any change in policy toward South Africa would mean; specifically, evaluation by the United States Joint Chiefs of Staff as to the effect of any action by the UN or by the United States on the military balance of power in southern Africa. Ambassador Goldberg was reported to have addressed the Joint Chiefs several times at President Johnson's order to explain the political significance of Southwest Africa. (Johannesburg *Sunday Times,* April 2, 1967, dispatch by the author.)

20. For example, if State wanted to "by-pass" the UN on some crucial issue in foreign policy and USUN insisted on UN participation, and if, indeed, the UN was then brought in not only as a participant but as an influential participant with the result that the United States policy aim received UN backing, one could then say this is a positive-sum game. Also see Thomas C. Schelling, *The Strategy of Conflict* (New York: Oxford University Press, paperback, 1963), p. 83.

"The most satisfactory answer to the zero-sum problem . . . is not one of either-or. In relatively democratic societies, there are probably very few empirical power situations even close to realizing the pure zero-sum situation where one player's gain precisely equals other players' losses. The contrary situation, which might be labeled a power-vacuum—where one player's gain implies absolutely no loss of any sort to any other players—may be, however just as infrequently found. Most empirical power situations in democratic political arenas seem to fall somewhere between these two extremes." Terry N. Clark, "The Concept of Power," *Southwestern Social Science Quarterly* (December 1967), p. 282.

21. Americans in the UN Secretariat have benefited from their UN relationship. Some years ago Ralph Bunche was discussed as a possible New York senatorial candidate. In spring 1967, Arthur Goldschmidt, for many years a ranking UN official, was appointed to the rank of Ambassador at the USUN.

22. Neal Gross, Ward S. Mason, Alexander W. McEachern, *Explorations in Role Analysis: Studies of the School Superintendency Role* (New York: John Wiley & Sons, 1964), p. 4.

23. Peter Woll, Introduction in *Public Administration and Policy* (New York: Harper and Row Torchbooks, 1966), p. 1.

24. A. J. Ayer, *Language, Truth and Logic*, p. 26. Quoted in D. A. Runes (ed.), *Twentieth Century Philosophy* (New York: Philosophical Library, 1943), p. 382.

2/ The UN and American Foreign Policy

Only the free peoples of the world can join the League of Nations. No nation is admitted to the League of Nations that cannot show that it has the institutions which we call free. No autocratic government can come into membership, no government which is not controlled by the will and vote of its people.[1]

So wrote Woodrow Wilson in his vain attempt to persuade the American people to support United States membership in the League of Nations. A quarter of a century later, President Roosevelt enunciated a different standard for membership to ensure that the new world organization would succeed where the other had failed.[2] Even though there was a wide American consensus that a world organization would be essential after World War

II, there were Europeans who were fearful that America would succumb to its historic isolationism. Trygve Lie, the UN's first Secretary-General, wrote:

> As I saw it, the challenging question for the future was how to secure the fullest possible United States participation in whatever international organizations might emerge from the wartime alliance.[3]

And if there was any single reason the UN headquarters came to the United States, it was, wrote Lie, "so that the concept of international cooperation could match forces on the spot with those of its arch-enemy, isolationism— utilizing at all times the American people's own democratic media."[4] While the concern about American isolationism was justified, it was hardly prophetic. Almost from the beginning of American entry into World War II, President Roosevelt had made it clear that an international organization would be the sine qua non of any postwar settlement. The Roosevelt philosophy was grounded on the belief that "in a democratic world, as in a democratic nation, power must be linked with responsibility and obliged to defend and justify itself within the framework of the general good."[5]

Support for the UN is now a cardinal tenet of most American statesmen. Few institutions, except the Fourth of July, have received so comprehensive a rhetorical commitment as has the UN. In 1946, President Truman said:

> The policy of the United States, as I told the General Assembly in New York October 23, 1946, is to support the

United Nations with all the resources that we possess . . .
not as a temporary expedient but as a permanent partnership.[6]

Senator Arthur H. Vandenberg told the UN General Assembly when he was a delegate:

I reassert, with whatever authority I possess, that, regardless of what political regime sits in Washington, you can count upon the wholehearted cooperation of the government of the United States in striving, through the United Nations, for a system of mutual defense against any aggression and for organizing peace with justice in a better, safer world.[7]

Secretary of State James F. Byrnes said, "We have pinned our hopes to the banner of the UN." His successor, George Marshall, said that "support for the UN is the cornerstone of our foreign policy." Dean Acheson said that "the foreign policy of the United States is based squarely upon the UN." President Eisenhower said that "[we are] a government that is committed irrevocably to the support of the UN."[8]

President Kennedy's pronouncement was on the same lofty plane:

In supporting the United Nations, we not only support the aims and ideals inscribed in our own Constitution, but we work to convert the high goals of our foreign policy into a living reality: the achievement of a world community of independent states living together in free association, in liberty and in peace.[9]

President Johnson has declared that "more than ever we support the United Nations as the best instrument yet devised to promote the peace of the world and to promote the well-being of mankind."[10] In even more forceful language, former Supreme Court Justice Arthur J. Goldberg has described the Charter as "a treaty to which we are party [and] is thus a part of supreme law of the United States under our Constitution."[11]

That these statements reflect strong pro-UN feeling by Americans can be seen from public opinion surveys. For example, in 1937 one poll showed that only 26 per cent of a sample favored American membership in the League of Nations. In May 1941, even though we were not yet in the war, 87 per cent were in favor of joining "a league of nations after the war."[12] In polls taken during World War II, "public support for joining an international organization varied between 64 and 95 per cent." In 1951, and through 1953, the polls showed a mean of 78 per cent of poll respondents in favor of remaining in the UN and a mean of 11 per cent for withdrawal. The remainder were in the "don't know; depends" category.[13] The study of one hundred national attitude surveys on the UN seems to show that support of the UN is unrelated to geographical factors, age groupings, political party affiliation. The only seemingly significant difference in responses arose from differences in education: the higher a person's educational attainment, the more pro-UN he was, but also (as of 1955) the more dissatisfied with the functioning of the UN.

More recent surveys have demonstrated that the UN continues to enjoy high favor in America. The Lou Harris survey for April 1966 reported that Americans favored by nearly 2 to 1 (50 per cent to 27 per cent) that the Vietnam war be turned over to a special three-man UN committee for arbitration and a decision binding on all parties.[14] In a discussion of these more recent polls, Seymour Martin Lipset said that

the strength of the sentiment to turn the war over to the United Nations may be seen in the fact that the only occasion recorded by the polls in which the group of respondents voicing an explicitly negative judgment of President Johnson far outweighed his supporters has been on this issue. These attitudes not only reflect ambivalent sentiments about U.S. participation in Vietnam, they also indicate the very strong positive feeling of the American people towards the United Nations. All the surveys have consistently indicated widespread popular support for the UN. . . . Almost all Americans seem to identify the UN with prospects for world peace and are willing to do anything to endorse it, including criticizing American foreign policy if the question is worded in such a way as to make the pro-UN response involve such criticism. [Emphasis added.][15]

The favorable American public attitude toward the world organization, as well as regional organizations such as the Organization of American States and the North Atlantic Treaty Organization, has visibly and practically affected American foreign policy and the establishment of machinery to implement that policy. Since 1944 "the United States has built up what is unquestionably the

23

most elaborate policy-making and policy-executive structure of any of the members of the United Nations."[16]
What this elaborate structure has accomplished in twenty-
two years of UN history has been to make the UN so
integral a part of American civilization and culture that
few Americans who would wish to be taken seriously in
politics would today dream of suggesting American withdrawal from the organization.[17]

Quite meaningful too is the fact that outstanding
Americans have regarded the UN assignment, whether as
Chief of Mission or as members of the Delegation to the
annual General Assembly, as rewarding enough to merit
resignation from other public positions or, in the case of
delegates, to take time from their duties in private life
to serve three or more active months at the UN.[18] Apart
from Senators and Representatives who have served,
Assembly delegates have included Mrs. Eleanor Roosevelt, Marian Anderson, Henry Ford II, Irene Dunne,
Channing Tobias, Dr. Charles Mayo, and George Meany.

A considerable body of literature exists to demonstrate
the value of the UN in fulfilling American foreign policy
aims. It is a literature to which analysts, such as
Robert Strausz-Hupé, director of the Foreign Policy
Research Institute, University of Pennsylvania, have made
affirmative contributions.[19]

Benjamin V. Cohen, a senior adviser to the United
States Delegation in the early UN days, says that the
existence of the world body has:

1. *Clearly caused the U.S. to justify and defend within the framework of UN principles and purposes its exercise of power.*

2. *Affected American policy "in re as well as in modo."*

3. *Broadened American foreign policy scope because it has made that policy more conscious and responsive to the political, economic and social problems which sooner or later must affect the interest of the U.S. as a world power.*

4. *Made the U.S. more quickly conscious and responsive to the effects of its foreign policy on world opinion.*[20]

For Richard N. Gardner, former Deputy Assistant Secretary of State for International Organizations, the UN was at its most effective October 1962 during the crucial confrontation week between the United States and the Soviet Union over the Cuban missile sites.[21] The UN fulfilled each of its three main functions:

(1) *As a place for debate, the United Nations enabled the United States to build support for its Cuban policy in the most rapid and effective way.*

(2) *As a place for negotiation, the UN was scarcely less important.*

(3) *Lastly, as a place for action, the UN demonstrated its peace-keeping potential for the future.*

Two passages in Sherman Adams' autobiography show the extent of UN involvement with American foreign policy during the Suez crisis. The first passage describes a top-level discussion among President Eisenhower's advisers during the Suez crisis and the consequent oil emergency in Britain and France. Adams writes:

> *[Arthur] Flemming asked what the reaction would be in the United Nations and among the Arab states when it became known that the United States government was relieving the oil shortage in Britain and France. [Herbert] Hoover [Jr.] said there would be no objections to the oil pool if it went into effect after the British and the French withdrew their forces from the Suez Canal zone. [George] Humphrey did not think that Hammarskjold would be agreeable unless the British and the French were in compliance with the United Nations' resolution. . . . Humphrey was hesitant about moving too fast. He insisted that Hammarskjold or someone else at the UN should first decide the question of compliance before we made any move.[22]*

And at a meeting of congressional leaders assembled at the White House Cabinet room, February 20, 1957, Adams writes:

> *Eisenhower stated flatly that he did not know how to protect American interests in the Middle East except through the United Nations. . . . [John Foster] Dulles told them that if Israel were allowed to defy the withdrawal order any longer, the basic principle of the United Nations forbidding any individual nation from taking the law into its own hands would become ineffective and worthless.[23]*

I am not prepared to argue that Eisenhower or his Cabinet officials were maintaining some grand moral position. At about the same time that the Administration was worrying about the UN's role in Suez, it was indicating a lesser concern about Soviet violations of UN resolutions dealing with the Soviet aggression against Hungary during October–November 1956. What may certainly be said is that it suited American foreign policy-makers at this specific time to give the UN or the Secretary-General a semblance of veto power over their actions. What may also be correct is that it was a lot easier for American public opinion, because of the UN, to accept United States rejection of its NATO allies, France and England, and even for Zionists to accept United States hostility toward Israel's aggression against Egypt.[24] And all this in an alliance *de convenance* with the Soviet Union! I am not suggesting that the UN was the sole reason for this twist of American policy. Eisenhower's popularity and the silence of the Democratic party made policy acceptance that much easier. I am suggesting that to act in the name of, and with the approval of, the UN made it all morally palatable.

My reason for going into such detail about the UN and American foreign policy is to lay the foundation for a study of the USUN. If American foreign policy were hostile to the UN, if the President and the Secretary of State were publicly to announce their distrust of the UN and were to threaten withdrawal, quite obviously the USUN would serve just as well from an extraterrestrial station as it does from First Avenue and 45th Street in New York. However, when a government so fervently endorses an international organization and when government spokesmen, privately and publicly, demonstrate that this endorsement is more than rhetorical commitment, it may follow that the agency and the actor assigned to implement that commitment have been endowed with a role which no other mission or chief of mission either to a host country or another international organization possesses legitimately and continuously.[25]

The uniqueness of the UN arises from the fact that from its inception it was *intended* to be unique, whether compared to the Achaean League, the Concert of Europe, or to the League of Nations. The UN's particular uniqueness, its difference from other international organizations, whether past or present, is due in part to the entry of large publics into contemporary politics, particularly in the area of foreign policy, whether it is picketing the UN, burning foreign embassies, or showing by their votes that they favor international organization. Since the UN is the focus of these open political efforts, it means that the UN–USUN–Washington triangle is the center of that aspect of world diplomacy which convenants openly. Washington, Moscow, and the UN's world public all took it for granted that the stage setting for the Cuban missile crisis of 1962 belonged not at SHAPE headquarters, not in the OAS, not in Moscow, but in the Security Council chamber on the East River, even though the UN could do very little when the two superpowers confronted each other.

The button was in the White House situation room, but the crisis moved automatically to the Security Council chamber without the slightest objection from anybody

—and Soviet Ambassador Valerian Zorin was Security Council President that October 1962.

In January 1968, the crisis engendered by the North Korean seizure of the USS *Pueblo* moved at American request to the Security Council. Legally, there was nothing the UN or any of its organs or functionaries could do. The move was, however, a useful tactic in "crisis management" since it gave the impression that something was happening and that the American government was not as helpless as it appeared to be when confronted by what the Secretary of State defined as "an act of war."

It is this fact of modern international life—that almost all world crises come to the UN with an automatic guarantee of media coverage—which gives the USUN its world visibility and the tremendous resources within its subsystems.[26] Our representatives to NATO, to the European Community organizations, or to OAS, let alone to the many other international organizations on which we are represented, have little of the autonomy or prestige which inheres in the USUN and its Chief. Because the Mission Chief lives in what might be regarded as the charismatic "UN atmosphere," the USUN is distinguished from other United States missions as the UN is distinguished from other international organizations.

Responsibilities upon the USUN have increased sharply in recent years as the UN membership has increased to include small countries, the ex-colonial minipowers. The UN–USUN–Washington triangle is the diplomatic capital not only for the Big Powers but also for the small countries. United Nations Ambassador George Ball has pointed out that minicountries that can hardly afford diplomatic representation in more than a few capitals are always represented at the UN. "Thus if an African nation has business with Japan or India or Brazil, it is more than likely these days to tell its mission in New York to talk to the Japanese or Indian or Brazilian delegation in New York."[27] In 1952, Leland M. Goodrich could write, and correctly so, that because the United States was the richest and most powerful single member in the UN, "no important action can be undertaken by the United Nations with any reasonable prospect of success in the face of United States opposition."[28] Today the statement would need redefinition, particularly the key words, "important" and "success." Until a few years ago, the United States had an automatic majority; but today, as one USUN observer told me: "This is no longer true. Our opposition doesn't insure defeat any more. Arm-twisting doesn't work. The U.S. role must be more subtle. Today if we want to win in the UN we must plan our strategy better, and more carefully."

Upon few other UN delegations are such heavy burdens imposed as on USUN. And they are particularly heavy because the UN has become the place to dump every kind of problem, particularly when immediate solutions are invisible or inconceivable. This is piled on over and above the serious war-and-peace questions with which the

UN is always seized. Between the end of World War I and the beginning of World War II, there were perhaps a half-dozen armed conflicts—Spain, Ethiopia, China, two in South America—which threatened world or hemispheric peace. According to Secretary of State Rusk, since the end of World War II there have been "379 instances of armed conflict, external and internal. And there have been at least 150 disputes or situations which so disturbed the world order as to engage the concern of the international community. In some 70 cases, the United Nations has become involved, either as principal peacemaker or in a complementary role."[29] (Rusk's cutoff date was October 1966.)

With the end of the United States nuclear monopoly, the proliferation of doomsday weaponry on what could be a pandemic scale, and with the ever-widening growth gap between the industrialized world and the Third World, lasting peace appears to be a fragile hope.[30]

Since the risks to world stability seem to increase each year, the workload of the UN expands, although there is wide agreement that for a variety of reasons it cannot really cope with all these risks. (For almost eight years, the war in Vietnam has been nonexistent so far as UN organs are concerned, excluding the Secretary-General, while the India-Pakistan war in 1965 and the 1967 Middle East war were settled at the UN.) Thus the work of USUN, one may suppose, will continue to increase to the same degree as that of the UN.

31

Notes

1. Franz B. Gross (ed.), *The U.S. and the UN* (Norman: University of Oklahoma Press, 1964), p. 4, quotes from *Woodrow Wilson's Case for the League of Nations* (Princeton: Princeton University Press, 1923), p. 64.

2. In his speech to the joint session of Congress, March 2, 1944, after the Yalta conference, F.D.R. said: "The Crimea conference . . . ought to spell the end of the system of unilateral action, the exclusive alliances, the spheres of influence, the balances of power, and all the other expedients that have been tried for centuries—and have always failed. We propose to substitute for all these, a universal organization in which all peace-loving nations will have a chance to join." Leo Pasvolsky, an adviser to Secretary of State Hull, wrote about the formation of the UN that "this time, the government of the United States, profiting by the unfortunate experience of twenty-five years earlier, was making every effort to go into negotiations for the creation of an international organization completely prepared technically and with the country united in support of the basic ideas which were put forward." Quoted by Quincy Wright (ed.), *A Foreign Policy for the United States* (Chicago: University of Chicago Press, 1947), p. 75.

3. Trygve Lie, *In The Cause of Peace* (New York: Macmillan, 1954), p. 57.

4. Ibid., p. 58.

5. U.S. President, 1932–1945 (Roosevelt), *State of the Union Message*, January 6, 1945.

6. U.S. Department of State Publication No. 2753, *Letter of Transmittal for the President's Report to the Congress on the United Nations*, 1946.

7. *The Private Papers of Arthur H. Vandenberg, Jr.* (New York: Houghton Mifflin, 1952), p. 317.

8. These quotations are from "American Policy Toward the UN—Some Bureaucratic Reflections, *International Organization*, Vol. XII (1958), *passim*.

9. John F. Kennedy, Preface to Adlai Stevenson, *Looking Outward*, Robert L. and Selma Schiffer (eds.) (New York: Harper and Row, 1961), p. xi.

10. U.S. President, 1963— (Johnson), *U.S. Participation in the UN*, Department of State Publication No. 7675, 1963, p. iv.

11. U.S. Department of State Publication No. 7733. A comparative view of the Charter comes from Richard N. Gardner, former Deputy Assistant Secretary of State for International Organization Affairs, who has written, "The Soviet Union has always seen the United Nations Charter essentially as a contract between rival states rather than as a constitution capable of organic growth in the service of a world community." (*In Pursuit of World Order: U.S. Foreign Policy and International Organizations* [New York: Praeger, 1964], p. 49.)

12. William A. Scott and Stephen B. Withey, *The United States and the United Nations: The Public View, 1945–55* (New York: Manhattan Publishing Co., 1958), p. 11.

13. *Ibid.*, p. 16, Table 5.

14. Seymour Martin Lipset, "Doves, Hawks and Polls," *Encounter*, XXVII, No. 4 (October 1966), 40 ff.

Findings such as these may account for the following Presidential press colloquy:

"Q. Mr. President, Secretary General U Thant made a speech yesterday in which he put forth the claim that the war in Vietnam is due to the desire of the Vietnamese people to have the same kind of freedom that we fought for in 1776. Could you explore for us your feelings?

"A. I don't agree with him, but I don't care to argue with a representative of the United Nations on his desire to give his viewpoint to our people."

(*New York Times*, August 1, 1967, p. 16.)

15. Lipset, *loc. cit.* To judge how extraordinary are the findings of these public opinion surveys, one should recall that "more than a year after the establishment of the United Nations, one-third of the adult population were not sufficiently aware of its existence to be able to give the simplest explanation of its purpose, even in such terms as 'to keep the peace' and as late a date as October 1948, one-quarter of the population were still in that position." (David Truman, *The Governmental Process* [New York: Knopf, reprinted 1965], p. 219.) Yet this finding should be paired with public opinion polls in 1947, 1951, and 1954 which showed that "the functions of the UN are in general better known than those of the US Department of State. In February 1953, only 41% of a national cross-section of adults was able to give approximately correct answers to the question 'Can you tell me what the main job is of the State Department, in Washington?'" (Scott and Withey, *op. cit.*, p. 32.) For a summary of how the UN was "sold" to the American public, see John Dickey, "The Secretary and the American Public," in Don K. Price (ed., for the American Assembly, Columbia University),

The "Other" State Department

The Secretary of State (Englewood Cliffs, N.J.: Prentice-Hall, 1960), pp. 146 ff.

16. Lincoln Bloomfield, *The United Nations and U.S. Foreign Policy* (Boston: Little, Brown, 1960), p. 257.

17. H. G. Nicholas, *The United Nations in Crisis* (Chatham House: International Affairs, July 1965), p. 443: "American support, both official and private, for the UN has been strong and, in the main, consistent over the twenty years since San Francisco. That the organization exists and functions at all *is due more to the United States than to any single nation.*" (Emphasis added.)

18. During his G.O.P. Vice-Presidential campaign in 1960, Lodge, who had served as a UN delegate to the 1950–51 General Assembly while a Senator before becoming USUN Chief, almost always began a speech with this sentence. "I come to you tonight after eight years in the UN where I spoke for all the nation . . . regardless of party." Tom Wicker, writing in *The New York Times*, said: "Mr. Lodge so often begins his speeches on this note for the simple reason the invariable response is long and prolonged applause, sometimes even a standing ovation. Mr. Lodge brings a ready-made personality—a fully-created image—to the voters." Quoted in William J. Miller, *Henry Cabot Lodge* (New York: James H. Heineman, Inc., 1967), pp. 323–324.

19. Strausz-Hupé says that (1) the UN provides a channel of diplomatic communications with the USSR, (2) its specialized agencies execute broad humanitarian projects, (3) some countries whose economic health is "vital to our objective" will shun bilateral aid, but will take it on a multilateral UN basis, (4) the UN can provide some peace enforcement without loss of face to the involved parties. (Franz B. Gross, [ed.], *op. cit.*, p. 20.)

20. Benjamin V. Cohen, "Impact of the United Nations on United States Foreign Policy," *International Organization*, V, No. 2 (May 1951), 280.

21. Gardner, *op. cit.*, pp. 73–74.

22. Sherman Adams, *Firsthand Report* (New York: Harper and Row, 1961), p. 264.

23. *Ibid.*, p. 282.

24. Eight years earlier this might not have been easy to accomplish. "At their national conventions in 1948," Robert A. Dahl has written, "both parties adopted pro-Israel planks. . . . Both presidential candidates were unwilling to neglect the possibility of securing votes on that issue. Ultimately the American delegation at the United Nations, which was then concerned with the Palestine problem, found it necessary to post-

34

pone all discussion of the problem until the election was over." (*Congress and Foreign Policy* [New York: Norton, 1964], p. 56.)

25. A mission can have moments of unusual autonomy quite legitimately, but it is ad hoc. For example, in July 1960 Ambassador Clare Timberlake, at Léopoldville (now Kinshasa), was given full authority to act as he saw fit by Secretary of State Christian Herter. Such authority was granted the American Ambassador because, as a result of the Force Publique mutiny against the Belgians and breakdown in social services, Washington–Léopoldville communications were slow and sometimes nonexistent. Since there was some apprehension that the Soviet Union might respond favorably to Premier Lumumba's request for Red Army troops to oust the Belgian military, Timberlake was told he could act without further instructions. That action envisioned a possible radio call to the U.S.S. *Wasp*, the aircraft carrier cruising off the Congo River mouth in the South Atlantic, to catapult its planes to prevent Soviet troop-carriers from landing and seizing Léopoldville. When, however, communications were restored, the Ambassador's emergency powers ended. This story is known personally to the author, who was in Léopoldville at the time.

26. The UN significance in the area of communication has become enormously important because of its geographical location. Had Kosygin not attended the UN General Assembly emergency session in New York in the summer of 1967, it might have been difficult and perhaps impossible to arrange in a few hectic days the United States-Soviet summit meeting at Glassboro, N.J. At critical moments in international life, precedence—who blinked first?—and physical arrangements may become so important that statesmen must act as humorless *protocolaires*. It is a valid assumption—without necessarily implying a value judgment—that the Johnson-Kosygin meeting came about because Kosygin was already in New York. He might for all kinds of reasons have been unable to go to Washington, D.C., or to Texas but something as anonymous internationally as Glassboro was apparently suitable. Since the UN has this continuing geographical significance, it would appear a justifiable conclusion that the USUN Chief draws increased geopolitical resources from his involvement in the UN subsystem. The early debates between Hanoi and Washington in Spring 1968 about a site for preliminary negotiations underscore the geopolitical problems in international negotiations. Secretary of State Rusk during mid-April 1968 sought "third party" influence with Hanoi to settle on a mutually acceptable place for the first meeting. The "third party" was UN Secretary-General U Thant, who received the suggestions through

Ambassador Goldberg. However, on at least one occasion known to this writer, the Ambassador told Rusk he would prefer to withhold a proposed message to Thant until he, Goldberg, had had a chance personally to discuss the subject with the President directly. The President was then (April 17) en route from Honolulu and could not be reached until the following day. Rusk accepted the delay.

27. *State Department Bulletin*, XLVI, No. 1190 (April 16, 1962), 638.

28. Leland M. Goodrich, "American National Interests and Responsibilities of United Nations Membership," *International Organization*, VI (1952), pp. 369–380. The quotation is on p. 378.

29. Department of State Publication No. 8163. Address given by Dean Rusk before the George C. Marshall Memorial Dinner of the Association of the United States at Washington, D.C., October 12, 1966. The citation begins on p. 5.

30. "The burden of demonstrating that the world will be less violent in the second half of the twentieth century than in the first half lies with those who believe that 2.8 billion people can modernize in relative comfort because 445 million have reached the relatively and perhaps only temporarily safe haven of social integration." (C. E. Black, *Dynamics of Modernization: A Study in Comparative History* [New York: Harper and Row, 1966], p. 151.) He also predicts that there will be ten to fifteen revolutions a year in the foreseeable future in the Third World.

3/ The United States Mission —Its Legal Structure

The United States Mission is officially defined as one which "resembles a United States Embassy in some respects, but it is on our soil and is accredited, not to a foreign government but to the United Nations."[1] The official residence of the Ambassador on the forty-second floor of the Waldorf-Astoria Towers on Park Avenue at 50th Street has on its door a replica of the Great Seal of the United States which bears the legend, "Embassy of the United States of America."

The statutory basis for American participation in the UN is to be found in the Participation Act of 1945, amended in 1949.[2] In addition, there were two Executive orders, both promulgated by President Truman to effectuate the Participation Acts. The law provides for the appointment by the President, with the advice and consent of the Senate, of the principal American representatives to the United Nations. The chief representative is given the rank of Ambassador "so as to counteract any notion that his office might operate independently of the President."[3]

The salary was specified at $20,000 annually (it is now $30,000) and in addition to his duties described, the law says that the Ambassador "shall perform such other functions in connection with the participation of the United States in the United Nations as the President may from time to time direct." A deputy representative was also provided for. Five representatives to the General Assembly are also to be appointed with the advice and consent of the Senate.[4] Members of the House and Senate may be appointed as representatives and alternates to attend the General Assembly. The President is also empowered to make other necessary appointments to provide for representation in other UN organs and agencies.

One clause provides that the President or Secretary of State may attend any meeting or session of any UN organ or agency. In such cases, the regular United States representative is displaced for that meeting or session. Section 3 of the bill has particular relevance to the peculiar status of the Mission in our foreign policy establishment:

Sec. 3. The representatives provided for in section 2 hereof, when representing the United States in the respective organs and agencies of the United Nations, shall, at all times, act in accordance with the instructions of the President transmitted by the Secretary of State unless other means of transmission is directed by the President, *and such representatives shall, in accordance with such instructions, cast any and all votes under the Charter of the United Nations.* [*Emphasis added.*]

Thus we have two provisions which establish a unique relationship between the President and the Ambassador to the UN: first, the President may direct him to perform "other functions"; second, the President may transmit instructions to the Ambassador and other representatives through "other means of transmission" than the Secretary of State. Obviously, any Presidential appointee may be assigned all kinds of duties within his competence and receive instructions in any fashion the President desires. Yet it was felt important that specific mention be made of these options in the Participation Act. A third provision is that the Ambassador "shall hold office at the pleasure of the President," which means he can be fired without a hearing or without stated reason.

Section 4 stresses the role Congress plays in United States participation in the UN by providing that the President must report to Congress, at least once a year, on United States-UN affairs. The House Foreign Affairs Committee report interpreted Section 4 thus:

Although the ratification of the Charter resulted in the vesting in the executive branch of the power and obligation to fulfill the commitments assumed by the United States thereunder, the Congress must be taken into close partner-ship and must be fully advised of all phases of our participa-tion in this enterprise.[5]

Section 5 empowers the President to join with other countries in applying enforcement measures short of armed force under Article 41 of the UN Charter, in deal-ing with particular disputes. Section 6 authorizes the President to negotiate military agreements with the Security Council under Article 43 of the Charter to make available to the Council the armed force necessary to maintain international peace and security. There are other aspects to Section 6 relating to the legislative intent which went into its drafting, but they are not relevant here, particularly since the issue has not yet arisen under Article 43. Finally, Section 7 deals with appropriations for United States payment of its share of UN expenses and with representation allowances for the Mission.

Because the UN is on American soil, the Mission has the responsibility to see to it that the Headquarters Agree-ment between the United States and the UN is suitably discharged. The House of Representatives (on December 10, 1945) and the Senate (on December 11) unani-mously voted to invite the UN "to locate the seat of the United Nations Organization within the United States."[6] The UN accepted the invitation in February 1946 and then began a search for a suitable site. In December 1946, John D. Rockefeller, Jr., offered $8.5 million to purchase the land on which the UN building complex rests today.

February 26, 1947, the offer was approved by Congress.[7]

On July 2, 1947, President Truman transmitted to Congress a proposed agreement between the United States and the UN dealing with the control and administration of the UN headquarters-to-be in New York City.[8] The agreement complements Article 104 of the Charter and Article 105.[9] The Headquarters Agreement, as it is called, grants the UN freedom from various types of domestic regulations; recognizes the inviolability of the UN area (just as was the case with the League of Nations in Geneva), but obligates the UN to prevent the area from becoming a refuge for people seeking to avoid arrest; bars federal, state, or local authorities from preventing transit to or from the UN district of persons with legitimate business with the UN; authorizes the UN to establish and operate radio facilities. The congressional concern with national security was covered in a new section to the joint resolution which declared:

Sec. 6. Nothing in the agreement shall be construed as in any way diminishing, abridging, or weakening the right of the United States to safeguard its own security and completely to control the entrance of aliens into any territory of the United States other than the headquarters district and its immediate vicinity, as to be defined and fixed in a supplementary agreement between the Government of the United States and the United Nations . . . and such areas as it is reasonably necessary to traverse in transit between the same and foreign countries. Moreover, nothing in section 14 of the agreement with respect to facilitating entrance into the United States by persons who wish to visit the headquarters district and do not enjoy the right of entry provided in section 11 of the agreement shall be construed to amend or suspend in any way the immigration laws of the United States or to commit the United States in any way to effect any amendment or suspension of such laws.[10]

Another law enacted was the International Organizations Immunities Act which extends certain privileges, exemptions, and immunities to public international organizations in which the United States participates and which are so designated under an Executive Order.[11]

Still another law to make the UN's existence easier was the International Organizations Procurement Act of 1947 whereby the United States government was authorized until December 31, 1946 (by amendment, this date was later extended at the request of Secretary-General Lie), to purchase all supplies and equipment for the UN on a reimbursable basis. This meant that the UN could avoid markups and high prices and benefit by the mass purchasing power of the government.[12]

The UN has defined its status in America with the statement that "under special agreement with the United States, certain privileges and immunities have been granted, but generally the laws of New York City, New York State and the United States apply."[13]

A contretemps under the Immunities Act arose during 1953 when the United States was attacked for refusing visas to foreign delegates from Communist-front organizations to attend certain UN meetings, in one case that of the Commission on the Status of Women, and in another that of the Economic and Social Commission on behalf of the Communist-dominated World Federation of Trade Unions. The American deputy representative, James J. Wadsworth, said the visas were withheld to safeguard American security under the reservation clause in Section 6, P.L. 387 (80th Congress), which authorized the Headquarters Agreement. The matter was put on the ECOSOC (Economic and Social Council) agenda for its 1954 session under the title: "Report of the Secretary-General on the results of negotiations with the Government of the United States with regard to access to UN headquarters of representatives of nongovernmental organizations with consultative status." However, Secretary-General Dag Hammarskjöld met with American authorities, and the problem was worked out with no further difficulties.[14]

Notes

1. Department of State Publication No. 74442, International Organization and Conference Series (35). Released December 1962 (rev.).

2. The UN Participation Act of 1945, enacted by the 79th Congress as Public Law 264, is described as "an ACT to provide for the appointment of representatives of the United States in the organs and agencies of the United Nations, and to make other provision with respect to the participation of the United States in such organization." The amended

Act was passed October 10, 1949, by the 81st Congress and is known as Public Law 341. The texts of the two laws are included in the volume published by the Senate Foreign Relations Committee called "A Decade of American Foreign Policy, 1941–49," *Sen. Doc. 123*, 81st Cong., pp. 156–162.

3. U.S. House of Representatives, *House Committee on Foreign Affairs, Report No. 1383.* 79th Cong., 1st Sess., December 12, 1945.

4. "As originally introduced in the Senate, the advice and consent of the Senate would not have been required with respect to these appointments. However, the bill was amended in the Senate to provide for Senate confirmation." Another amendment introduced barred any compensation for members of Congress when serving as members of the United States Delegation.

5. Report No. 1383, *op. cit.*

6. U.S. House of Representatives, *House Concurrent Resolution No. 75,* 79th Cong., 1st Sess., 1945.

7. Congress enacted an amendment to the Internal Revenue Code which exempted the Rockefeller gift from federal estate and federal gift tax. Lacking such an amendment, Rockefeller would have had to pay a gift tax ranging from $3.7 to $4.8 million (see U.S. Department of State Bulletin, Vol. XVII, No. 434, October 26, 1947, p. 797, footnote 15).

8. *H.R. Doc. 376,* 80th Cong., 1st Sess. (1947), pp. 1–2.

9. The relevant passages in Article 104 stipulate, "The Organization shall enjoy in the territory of each of its Members such legal capacity as may be necessary for the exercise of its functions and the fulfillment of its purposes." Article 105 stipulates, in part, "The Organization shall enjoy in the territory of each of its Members such privileges and immunities as are necessary for the fulfillment of its purposes" and the General Assembly "may make recommendations with a view to determining the details of the application" of this provision.

10. *S. Rep. 559,* 80th Cong., 1st Sess. (1947), pp. 5–6, explains the intent and background of this provision. The Headquarters Agreement is Senate Joint Resolution 144, which passed the House and the Senate July 26, 1947, authorizing the President to effectuate the agreement.

11. "The absurd anomaly persists that the host country has still not acceded to the General Convention on Privileges and Immunities, designed to give the UN quasi-diplomatic status, but with certain minor, irksome exceptions the substance of the convention has been incorporated in the Headquarters Agreement ratified in 1947." H. G. Nich-

olas, *The United Nations as a Political Institution* (New York: Oxford University Press, 1963), p. 180.

12. Many useful texts in these matters are to be found in Walter H. Zeydel and Waldo Chamberlin (compilers), *Enabling Instruments of Members of the United Nations. Part I, The United States of America* (New York: Carnegie Endowment for International Peace, 1951).

13. "In New York, the number of representatives [to the UN] possessing immunity is 1458; of these 264 are Soviet bloc nationals including 116 U.S.S.R. representatives." (*New York Times,* January 21, 1967, letter from J. Edgar Hoover to Secretary Rusk.)

14. *International Organization,* VII (1953), 394, 539. The opening day ceremonies of the 1967–1968 General Assembly were enlivened by Cuba, whose spokesman charged that United States Customs had refused to allow entry of "an undetermined number of wooden crates" without inspection. Ambassador Goldberg said that there was no violation of the Headquarters Agreement since the Cubans had not claimed the crates were diplomatic baggage. The matter was interred with U Thant for adjudication. U.S. Delegation to the General Assembly, Press Release No. 135 (September 19, 1967).

4/ The UN and Multilateral Diplomacy: Social and Political

The USUN is only one of several permanent United States missions attached to international organizations in different parts of the world.[1] None of them compare with the USUN in renown, importance, prestige, influence, and strategic location. The last attribute, which is subsumed in the UN's universality, is particularly valuable to governments; that is, experienced American diplomats can, in a matter of hours, by judicious phone calls and private chats on the second-floor Delegates' Lounge of the General Assembly building, come up with a useful report on world reaction to some particular foreign policy matter. Andrew Cordier, dean of Columbia University's Faculty of International Affairs and long-time UN ranking official, told the writer:

The USUN is so institutionalized that it can assess reactions of all UN members quickly and can therefore say to the State Department that in the opinion of the Mission, the American position ought to be thus-and-so on a given issue. The great function of a UN mission is to keep its foreign office informed of the temper of the aggregate membership of the United Nations on central issues.[2]

It is easy for delegates to meet and talk to each other around the UN buildings, without need for appointments or specific time allotments. In short, there is at this Parliament of Man greater informality of relationships than is the case in world capitals where diplomats are normally insulated from each other by sheer geography or by protocol within the capital city. It has even been suggested, and not always facetiously, that UN diplomacy would be aided immeasurably if the meeting-rooms were torn down and more corridors were designed in their stead; most decisions, it is argued, are made in private conversations in the corridors, and very little is decided at the meetings.[3] In the era of democracy and constitutionalism, corridor diplomacy may be a variant of what in the seventeenth and eighteenth centuries was called "boudoir diplomacy," minus the discreet pleasures.

These environmental qualities strike visitors to the UN as something quite extraordinary:

47

It was not until I began making regular visits to the great glass tower glittering above the East River that I started to grasp the intensity of the UN life. It was a world of its own, separate, self-contained and in chronic crisis, where a dozen unrelated emergencies might explode at once, demanding immediate reactions across the Government and decisions (or at least speeches) in New York. It had its own ethos, its own rules, and its own language. . . . It had its own social life, an endless and obligatory round of evening receptions, where American non-attendance might be taken as an insult and lose a vote on an important resolution.[4]

This prose of Arthur Schlesinger's understates what the UN "living system" is really like: the astonishing way rumors and gossip can sieve through the tightest security net, the gadding about by newspapermen and diplomats from reception to reception during the opening weeks of an Assembly session, and the importance (not, however, cosmic) attached by members of the UN subsystem to these receptions.[5] Secrets at the UN are hard to keep because of the immediacy with which events lead to decisions (or speeches). When the Egyptian Ambassador whispers to nonpermanent members of the Security Council at the moment when the United States is seeking inscription of the Vietnam issue, what he is whispering into the ears of his colleagues at the Council table is no secret. In a matter of hours, an American diplomat has notified the Egyptian diplomat what he and his government think of such unseemly lobbying against inscription, even if it is unsuccessful.[6]

Other aspects of UN social life were described by James N. Hyde, a former Mission official:

> Less formal meetings of the delegates occur constantly. The cocktail party, luncheon or dinner are occasions when information is exchanged, key people assemble to work on a draft or "trial balloons" are sent up. These social occasions make the delegation members' day a long one, but they are where much of the work of an international conference is done.[7]

Hyde reminds us that at the prescribed dinner of the President of the Security Council in June 1951 began one of the first exploratory conversations between Soviet Ambassador Malik and United States Deputy Representative Ernest Gross about a Korean armistice. It is entirely possible that had there been no Council dinner the conversations would have taken place elsewhere and, perhaps, between different diplomats. To say that the Korean armistice and the Council dinner are related may be one more example of a *post hoc propter hoc* fallacy—probably the commonest fallacy found in writings on international affairs. Yet some observers of and participants in the UN system feel that these social events have an important influence in the UN.[8]

Deputy Representative Gross, who served throughout four of the UN's most crucial years, has pointed out that the UN presence was helpful in matters outside the UN jurisdiction: "the channel between Soviet Ambassador Malik and myself would be often open." For example, before John Foster Dulles undertook the negotiations, at

President Truman's request, for a Japanese peace treaty, Dulles wanted to know the Soviet attitude toward such a treaty. Gross thereupon set up a meeting between Malik and Dulles, because "it was easy to meet in New York; it caused no comment." Malik and Gross frequently met in the Delegates' Lounge before or after meetings, Security Council dinners, dinners given by friends, official and unofficial, "and it was constant":

> I don't know of anybody I've ever been associated in diplomacy with whom I had more and longer talks than with Malik, frequently until three or four in the morning.[9]

The United Nations exemplifies an *aperçu* of Robert Michels, that "organization is the weapon of the weak in their struggle with the strong."[10] This view is explicated by Inis L. Claude, Jr., in a description of the UN Charter as representing "not the triumph of the unrealistic concept of equality, but a compromise between the claims of great and small states for status and formal power to participate in decision-making processes."[11] Nevertheless, some viewers look upon the UN as the ultimate unreality in diplomacy. Bernard Crick has written:

> The UN is not a political assembly because it is not a sovereign assembly. There are, strictly speaking, no politicians at the UN—merely ambassadors, statesmen, delegates [who] depend on instructions . . . a politician is not bound by daily instructions. Where government is impossible, politics is impossible—International diplomacy is "quasi-politics."[12]

The voting procedure had led some scholars, like Raymond Aron, into gentle derision of the UN even though he concedes that General Assembly votes have consequences because "democratic states are more sensitive to the judgments of world opinion and of their friends than are states of the Soviet type, which are always able to justify their actions, however cruel they may be, by a metaphysics of history."[13] While UN voting may be "a concept alien to the traditional system for the management of international relations," it necessarily influences USUN policies.[14]

The voting and roll-call aspect of the UN is but one of the "numbers" games which complicate the USUN's assignment, particularly since the Mission is an actor in several subsystems, but principally in the UN and the State Department subsystems. This "numbers" game can lead to strains among three actors—USUN, State, and UN—and to difficulties in arriving at compromise. Let me quote from an interview with an official of long experience at USUN:

The USUN has to think in terms of popularity, votes. It has to keep thinking of how it will win out when it comes to a vote. The prospect of being in a minority is an unpopular idea, and you are going to try to avoid that even at the expense of taking a position which implies something derogatory to the people down at State.

I asked for an example of just this sort. The American diplomat answered:

Take the fuzzily worded resolution on nonintervention. That's not the sort of resolution we'd draft or support, but we're afraid of being in a minority. It was introduced by the Soviet Union and was interpreted to mean an attack on our Vietnam policy. The Department fears that such a resolution would come to haunt us. Nevertheless we wanted to get on board because we [USUN] argued that if the United States votes for the resolution, it can't mean Vietnam. Even abstaining wasn't good enough, although the UK did abstain; but everybody else voted for it.[15]

The USUN official put his finger on the problem when he said:

This desire not to be caught in a minority is natural to any parliamentary situation. State isn't worried particularly, or, let's say, it's less worried than the USUN. We up here [New York] must explain to other delegations that we regard the proposed resolution as a stupid statement, but you can't explain it if a hundred delegates are for it. Just think, we had in the First Committee ten days of debate, and that's not including behind-the-scenes consultations! New York saw it in terms of the UN and didn't want to be on the defensive. The Department saw it, as is its inclination, not so much in terms of UN, but in terms of the general usefulness of such exercises and the legal problems for State.

One can say with the benefit of hindsight that the USUN-State Department bargaining relationship is inevitable. When Congress, glowing with a rarely visible transcendental bipartisanship, passed the law setting up a special agency, the USUN, to administer the American relationship to the UN Charter, it introduced a new actor into the foreign policy-making machine, little anticipating the latent consequences.[16] Here was a brand new institution in government for which there was neither definition nor description and thus no way of measurement of resources and boundaries.

Yet it may be asked whether there was a real need for a USUN. After all, the Constitution provides that the President "shall nominate, and, by and with the advice and consent of the Senate, shall appoint ambassadors."[17] The President could quite simply have asked the State Department to send him a list of its top career officers, and once the Charter was ratified, he could have appointed one of them as Ambassador to the UN without the dramatic scenario. The appointee could have worked out of a small State Department office in Washington, flown up a couple of days a week to New York, followed instructions, and in general behaved like a good career officer.

Instead we have a USUN in New York representing one of the biggest operations within the foreign policy-making system. What once had been a legitimated hierarchical structure within the State Department was affected by the intercalation not only of a USUN which became an actor in its own right but also of the UN itself which draws its authority from the fact that it is "accepted," in the same way that the universe was once accepted by Margaret Fuller. I would explain what has happened this way:

The "Other" State Department

When a State joins the UN, it definably foregoes or is prepared to forego a certain amount of its national sovereignty or autonomy. (This is truer of nontotalitarian countries than totalitarian, because the former are involved with interested publics whose opinions matter.) The surrender of some sovereignty to the UN even on a contingent basis (that is, on the quality and quantity of will of UN member nations) accrues to the UN subsystem; for example, to the Secretary-General, who can magnify his role (as in Suez or the Congo), or to the General Assembly, which can magnify its role (Uniting for Peace resolution).

Since the very concept of the UN implies surrender of some percentage of autonomy, the delegations can either enforce or disallow this surrender; that is, they can maximize or minimize the percentage of autonomy. Although a member nation may wish to pull back or to diminish the surrender of some sovereignty—as in the Connally amendment on World Court jurisdiction—its formal commitment to the Charter means diminution of autonomy in some degree. Thus USUN, like other delegations operating within a democratic system, is sometimes in the middle of a continuing bargaining process between the UN and the State Department, and sometimes the UN is in the middle between USUN and the State Department.[18] In other words, there are cases where the USUN is resisting the State Department subsystem which USUN inhabits. This conflict (for when the bargaining pressures reach the irresistible-immovable stage, one can describe that state as conflict) became inevitable or was built into the USUN system when, first, the UN Charter was ratified by Congress and, second, when Congress created the USUN as an institution with its own nomenclature and function, not living merely the life of an independent agency or as an adjunct of a Cabinet department.

The USUN's unique status has been accepted or at least understood by Congress. For example, Senators Hickenlooper and Mansfield, delegates to the General Assembly in 1959, reported that relationships between the State Department and "New York" were causing American participation to be "cumbersome and slow to respond to changing situations." They concluded:

If policy is to be pursued effectively in a General Assembly which includes over 80 other nations—nations whose differing views as well as idiosyncrasies of their representatives must be reckoned with—the Ambassador and the members of the permanent mission must have a measure of freedom for parliamentary maneuver.[19]

The dominant and most visible characteristic of the UN is what has been called "multilateral diplomacy [which] is marked by a codification process as a result of being subject to an agenda, debate and a formal vote. These require a degree of consistency, clarity and explainability that points towards logic and rigidity. The single most important check on multilateral diplomacy is the recourse to bilateral diplomacy."[20] The bilateral aspect of UN

55

diplomacy may be one way, and perhaps the only way, by which a Secretary of State may effectively assert his authority, his power of command, over a too independent USUN Chief, although this has not been stated publicly. Secretary Rusk has said, however, that

the General Assembly also has become the world's greatest switchboard for bilateral diplomacy. . . . In New York last Fall [1963] in a period of eleven days, I conferred with the foreign ministers or heads of governments of 54 nations.[21]

I am unsure, as indeed Sir Harold Nicolson most certainly would be unsure, what seeing fifty-four statesmen accomplished in what could only have been a short time interval for a busy Secretary of State; but if the Secretary had not seen them all, it might have caused difficulties, especially as they were all assembled in New York.[22]

Secretary Rusk feels quite strongly on the subject of being in constant contact with his opposite numbers. Recently, testifying before the Jackson subcommittee of the United States Senate, he said:

This [travel burden] is not just a problem for the Secretary of State. It is a problem for all foreign ministers. . . . I have discussed this problem with my colleagues, the other foreign ministers. . . . One of the advantages we do have which is convenient to the Secretary of State for geographic reasons, results from the fact that foreign ministers are in the habit of attending, more and more frequently, the first portion of the General Assembly of the United Nations. I think that where they are together, various groupings of them can con-

sult each other and individuals can see each other, which may serve to take the place of at least some of the travel.[23]

Ambassador Richard Pedersen, whose long service with the USUN is highly regarded in the State Department, prefers the phrase "parliamentary diplomacy" to "multilateral diplomacy" because, as he says, "the techniques of private negotiation are strongly influenced by the fact that a parliamentary test is intended before a final decision is taken."[24] Much has been written about parliamentary or multilateral diplomacy and its putative advantages over traditional bilateral diplomacy.[25] Philip C. Jessup, one-time UN ambassador and now a judge at the International Court of Justice, has defined parliamentary diplomacy as

the negotiation of solutions of international problems within the framework and through the procedures of an organized body acting under established rules of procedure, such as the General Assembly of the United Nations. The General Assembly, and indeed the whole United Nations complex with its permanent missions and its special committees, are today a part of the normal processes of diplomacy, that is of negotiation.[26]

Elsewhere he has said that

in contrast to the traditional type of bilateral diplomatic negotiations, a negotiation carried on in a parliamentary body with established rules of procedure introduces new factors in which the representatives of States frequently have to adjust

57

their positions to developments arising in the course of debate.[27]

Multilateral diplomacy has an arithmetical concomitant. The UN Twentieth Session listed 100 agenda items which, using Adlai Stevenson's formula, meant at least 11,600 national positions by 116 UN members. Stevenson created this formula when there were 110 UN members:

> *The task of the United States Mission to the UN is simple; merely to make sure that those 11,000 decisions are compatible with the national interest—while everyone else is trying to make sure that they are compatible with their national interest. [Emphasis in text.]*[28]

A more recent view of multilateral diplomacy in American foreign policy came from Ambassador Goldberg, who insisted that "the multilateral framework of the UN" made possible the negotiation of a treaty governing the use and exploration of outer space, including the moon and other celestial bodies. This "multilateral" environment, he said, worked because:

1. It "encouraged" the United States and the Soviet Union, as the space powers, to "be more forthcoming than they otherwise might have been."

2. It obliged the two space powers "to take account of the legitimate interests of other countries."

3. "In the light of the Vietnam war and the Sino-Soviet split, the fact that the space negotiations took place in the United Nations made it less difficult for the Soviet Union to make an agreement."[29]

The growth of multilateral diplomacy was remarked upon a few years after the UN birth by the unnamed author of Chapter 10 in the Woodrow Wilson Foundation Study on American foreign policy.[30] He pointed out that extensive participation by the United States in international bodies meant decisions and commitments "comparable in importance to those which have traditionally been considered suitable only for treatment by treaty procedure." He offered five features as unique in multilateralism:

1. The international bodies are permanent or semipermanent with periodic service for American representatives and staffs.

2. The agenda often is of major importance to the broad political and security interests of the United States.

3. United States representation is necessarily elaborate and in some instances considerably in excess of the organizational strength of the Washington office from which instructions are received.

4. In some instances, the United States may be committed to a particular policy by a majority of the international body even though the United States may be opposed to that policy.

5. "The mode of operation is such as to make it unavoidable that the United States representative must function at times either on his own initiative or after only the most cursory check with Washington."

That author put his finger on the dilemma which confronts State Department and USUN officials: the differing outlook between both groups about the same policy. United States participation in the UN involves

assignment of a portion of the policy-making function to a number of people outside the regular and traditional policy-making center of the Department of State—to the representative on the Security Council, to the members of our Delegation to the General Assembly and to the members of their staffs and the staff of the Bureau of United Nations Affairs in the Department of State. The significance of this is greatly heightened by the marked differences in atmosphere and outlook which often separate these people from the old established divisions of the Department and from the Foreign Service in general. [*Emphasis added.*]

The effect of this multilateralism is ideological, namely the importance attached by United Nations circles, whether American or foreign, "to the United Nations as an institution rather than just a forum of diplomacy."

Aside from ideological conceptions, "few people can be long associated with United Nations headquarters without being affected by the symbolism and spirit which tend to give it its own meaning and its own institutional existence."[31] In other words, these participants—or one might call them UN loyalists—have founded their interest in the UN "upon a wider basis than policy thinking in the confined precincts of the Department of State itself."

The UN's ideological foundation is the Charter. It is an ideological document, like the Declaration of Independence or the Communist Manifesto. It contains a set of integrated doctrines which make demands upon national sovereignty, and it presents underlying theories about war and peace and their causes. The Charter and the UN "living system" influence United States foreign policy in the same way the Constitution informs the American ethos on civil rights, democratic freedoms, Presidential power, the Supreme Court. By definition, therefore, the USUN is part of this UN ideology and of its documentation in a fashion which no other American diplomatic mission could possibly accept. The American Embassy in Paris is no more ideologically involved with Gaullism than the American Embassy in Damascus with Ba'athism or in Madrid with Falangism. Our various regional missions may be sympathetic to the European Communities or they may, in the case of NATO or OAS, share their pattern of ideological development; yet they are necessarily limited in assignment and commitment. The Soviet Union and the East European lands are barred from NATO and Cuba from the OAS.

In other words, the UN envisions a universality of membership (the United States position on Chinese representation could, in a technical sense, be regarded as aberrational), while other international bodies with which the United States is related are either without ideology, like the International Whaling Commission (to which the United States paid affiliation fees of $840 in 1965), or purely functional within the UN system of specialized agencies.

I have said that "the Charter and the UN 'living system' influence our foreign policy," thus raising questions such as:

1. What is "influence" in an international setting? Is it the same thing as accessibility?

2. How does one know who influences whom? How does one measure influence?

3. Is influence in an international system ever measurable?

4. What does the Charter influence the United States to do which it would or would not do in the absence of such a document?

Robert Dahl[32] has pointed out that in principle it is possible to determine the existence and direction of influence, while in practice "it is often difficult to find out who influences whom." Even more difficult is it to determine the duration, the time span, of influence, if it exists.

One can make out a strong case for UN influence on American foreign policy, without necessarily suggesting drastic alteration or reversal of any particular policy.[33] One can make out a good case for United States influence on UN "foreign policy," as well.

The difficulty in tracing influence and interactions among subsystems and between actors is that nothing stands still in international affairs.

In discussing UN influence in the United States, I am mindful of the fact that the UN's development may be affected by an observable growth in regionalism, or, in the words of Walt W. Rostow, "regional cooperation—within a framework of global collective security and common efforts in development, is likely to grow." Economic and political regional organizations, said Rostow, or regionalism "has thus commended itself to the United States as a way of permitting us to shift away from the disproportionate bilateral relations inherent in a large power working with smaller powers."[34] This movement, perhaps another form of "by-passing the UN," could conceivably attenuate UN influence on American foreign policy.[35] Yet when in the same speech we read (page 5) that "through persistent effort in the United Nations we have de-fused many small crises and choked off many episodes of violence which would have provoked major conflict," we have some confirmation that the UN does interact with American foreign policy.

So long as the Big Powers, and particularly the United States and USSR, regard it as useful to bring certain war-and-peace issues to the UN or to use the organization's machinery for other purposes, it means that major international questions will end up before the UN in some fashion. Another development may, however, in time detract from the UN's influence. The war-and-peace issues which have hitherto been the UN's "central concerns" may be changing with the admission of new states which, as Joseph E. Johnson has suggested, are outside the main stream of world politics:

And the concerns of the new states do not involve, as a matter of primary interest, the achievement of international order and stability. They involve, rather, the substantiation of national independence and the assertion of the international power to which the new states feel entitled by virtue of their numbers.[36]

In the meantime, the important *public* focus is the UN. For example, a number of world capitals were involved in the Suez crisis: Cairo, London, Paris, Tel Aviv, Moscow, and Washington; yet the main public focus was on the General Assembly and on the travels of Dag Hammarskjöld during October and November 1956. Assembly debates and Hammarskjöld's secret meetings with various protagonists seemed to be more real than the Sinai Desert. I am not arguing that issues like Suez, Kashmir, Cyprus, Aden, Israel, Cuba, and Vietnam have been or can be settled on the basis of "UN influence." I am saying that when these issues move in and out of the UN, they establish a UN presence in world politics and by so doing help organize world opinion, not as a monolithic entity, but as a force which must figure at the intergovernmental negotiating table. This is an aspect of multilateralism in diplomacy, through which the USUN (and other missions to a lesser degree) becomes a multilateral actor. In turn, the USUN Chief becomes a multilateral ambassador. Or, as Goldberg was quoted as saying after he had seen for the first time the 193-page official UN delegations' roster, "My God, I'm like a lawyer with 116 clients."[37]

In this chapter I have sought to describe the attributes which have contributed to the USUN's unique subsystem—unique when compared to other United States missions, whether they are in a single host country or in an international environment. I have also pointed out why the qualities of multilateral diplomacy and this UN subsystem affect the USUN and the State Department, so that they may be compelled to be on opposite sides of the fence, even though their mutual dependence continues.

Some of my statements, admittedly, are not empirically measurable since there are oscillations which make measurement difficult. Despite proposed tests, say, for "influence," finally there is no satisfactory test in a dynamic, interacting system with a multiplicity of actors and a profusion of roles for each of the actors, few of whom have acceptable precedents by which to perform.[38] In international affairs, the difficulties are compounded because all we know is what we know: a speech on international law, an off-the-record interview, a quasi-secret document. *More often we do not know what there is to know.* We may know the output without knowing all the inputs and the conversion process. Thus the testing or measurement apparatus for "influence" may be flawed at the outset.[39] In this connection, Ralf Dahrendorf has suggested that on occasion we may be dealing "with 'meta-theoretical' decisions which determine the direction of analysis with respect to specific problems without being part of this analysis themselves."[40]

Notes

1. Permanent missions sit in Geneva representing the United States at the European office of the UN, at the UN Economic Committee for Europe (ECE), the International Labor Organization, World Health Organization, International Telecommunications Union, World Meteorological Organization, and, most recently, the UN Conference on Trade and Development (UNCTAD). Then there are permanent missions to the European Communities and liaison missions with UNESCO in Paris, Food and Agriculture Organization in Rome, International Civil Aviation Organization in Montreal. A full report on United States participation in these and other agencies is to be found in U.S. House of Representatives, "United States Contributions to International Organizations," H.R. *Doc. 455*, 89th Cong., 2d Sess., June 27, 1966. The United States contributed a total of $326 million to seventy-one international organizations and programs in the fiscal year 1965. This figure covers only contributions to multilateral organizations, that is, those with three or more governmental members. Bilateral organizations are not included, nor are the large international financial organizations. On November 14, 1967, President Johnson announced that he would shortly create a United States Mission to the Organization of American States "with a staff expanded and structured to meet the growing responsibility of the organization." It would mean promotion of Sol M. Linowitz from the President's personal representative to the OAS to ambassador and mission chief. Linowitz, former board chairman of Xerox, is, like Ball and Goldberg, non-career, and no doubt will complicate the life of the Assistant Secretary of State for Latin American Affairs, should he lack Mr. Linowitz's access to the President. (*New York Times*, November 16, 1967.)

2. Interview with Andrew Cordier, April 10, 1967.

3. Ambassador Philip C. Jessup and Soviet Ambassador Jacob A. Malik met unobtrusively in the corridors of the Lake Success UN complex several times in 1949 to discuss settlement of the Berlin blockade. (Daniel S. Cheever, "Role of the United Nations in the Conduct of United States Foreign Policy," *World Politics* [April 1950], p. 396.) While these details have an air of melodrama about them, it is true that the very naturalness or seemingly accidental quality of a meeting between two adversaries at the UN can easily conceal serious negotiations.

4. Arthur M. Schlesinger, Jr., A *Thousand Days. John F. Kennedy in the White House* (New York: Houghton Mifflin, 1965), p. 411.

5. During his spring 1960 visit to the UN, Nikita Khrushchev caused considerable annoyance to several Western delegations because they could not find out sufficiently in advance which of several member state receptions he would attend in the evening. Had they known which receptions Khrushchev would attend, Western delegations, involved in competitive "cultural coexistence," would have been able to assign ranking delegation members to attend them as well. It was particularly annoying when Khrushchev showed up most unexpectedly at the reception tendered by Sylvanus Olympio, President of the Republic of Togo, in two small rooms at the Plaza Hotel. The ranking United States official at the reception when Khrushchev arrived with his entourage was the press officer. It is all part of UN "gamesmanship" in a system where causes and effects are not predictable. The incident described here is autoptic.

6. This episode occurred in the winter of 1965 and led to a protest by the United States to Cairo on the grounds that when a Security Council permanent member is barred from inscribing an issue on the Council agenda—so that it can be debated and no more—the future of the UN is imperiled. This episode was told the writer by Goldberg.

7. James N. Hyde, "U.S. Participation in the UN," *International Organization*, X, No. 1 (February 1956), 31.

8. John G. Hadwen and Johan Kaufman, *How United Nations Decisions Are Made*, 2d rev. ed. (Dobbs Ferry, N.Y.: Oceana Publications, 1962), p. 58. That this social activity may become a little ludicrous can be seen in Cecil V. Crabb, Jr., *American Foreign Policy in the Nuclear Age*, 2d ed. (New York: Harper, 1965), p. 410: "In a recent Senate appropriations hearing, Ambassador Henry Cabot Lodge, head of the U.S. delegation to the UN, pleaded for a dining room table with forty seats because 'that is where I try to line up the votes. Under UN rules, an important question must receive a two-thirds vote,' he went on to explain to the Senators, 'and you know how hard that is. If you get a man up and give him a good dinner and get him into a good frame of mind, you can get a good deal more done.'" (Cited from U.S. Senate, Subcommittee of the Committee on Appropriations, 85th Cong., 1st Sess., no page reference.)

9. Ernest A. Gross, *Oral History Project*, Columbia University. Transcript, p. 16.

10. Robert Michels, *Political Parties* (New York: Dover, n.d.), p. 21.

11. Inis L. Claude, Jr., *Swords Into Plowshares*, 3d rev. ed. (New York: Random House, 1964), p. 125.

12. Bernard Crick, *In Defense of Politics*, rev. ed. (London: Penguin Books, 1964), p. 29.

13. Raymond Aron, *Peace and War: A Theory of International Rela-*

tions (New York: Doubleday, 1966), p. 558. On page 559 he writes that "since a motion of the General Assembly requires a two-thirds majority, the super powers are obliged to court the small powers in order to gain the promise of a favorable vote. Equals of the super powers according to the law of the assembly, the small powers can pride themselves on using their votes to make historical decisions."

14. Claude, *op. cit.*, p. 11. He further writes that "much of the thinking about the international voting question has rested upon the assumptions borrowed from the outside, rather than on principles developed with specific reference to the requirements of international organizations. Thus the equalitarianism of traditional international law, the majoritarianism of democratic philosophy and the elitism of European great power diplomacy have been transferred to the sphere of international organization to serve as competing elements in shaping the approach to international decision-making." (Chapter 7, "The Problem of Voting.")

15. The interviewee cannot be identified by name. The resolution he referred to is to be found in United Nations, *General Assembly Document No. 2131* (20th Gen. Assembly, 1965), p. 11.

16. To get a sense of how urgently Congress felt about the UN and the need for a USUN, see U.S. House of Representatives, *House Committee on Foreign Affairs, Report No. 1383*, 79th Cong., 1st Sess., December 12, 1945, to accompany S. 1580. The report quotes from the Senate Foreign Relations Committee report of July 1945.

17. *Constitution of the United States*, Article II, Section 2.

18. See Chapter 6, "Where Is the Real Power," which in part deals with the Hammarskjöld interventions between Ambassador Lodge and Secretary Dulles.

19. U.S. Senate, "Observations of the United Nations," *Sen. Doc.* 26, 86th Cong., 1st Sess., pp. 6–7.

20. *United States Foreign Policy: Its Organization and Control*, Report of Study Group for the Woodrow Wilson Foundation (New York: Columbia University Press, 1952), p. 172.

21. Andrew Cordier and Wilder Foote (eds.), *The Quest for Peace* (New York: Columbia University Press, 1965), p. 74.

Secretary Rusk is credited with having coined the phrase "parliamentary diplomacy" in 1955. (Dean Rusk, "Parliamentary Diplomacy —Debate vs. Negotiation," *World Affairs Interpreter*, XXVI, No. 2 [Summer 1955], 121–122. Cited in David A. Kay (ed.), *The United Nations Political System* [New York: John Wiley & Sons, 1967], p. vi.)

22. Sir Harold Nicolson has written: "Nothing could be more fatal than the habit (the at present fatal and pernicious habit) of personal

contact between the statesmen of the world. It is argued, in defense of this pastime, that the foreign secretaries of the nations get to know each other. This is an extremely dangerous cognisance. Personal contact breeds, inevitably, personal acquaintance and that, in its turn, leads in many cases to friendliness: there is nothing more damaging to precision in international relations than friendliness between contracting parties. Locarno, not to mention Thoiry, should have convinced us of the desirability of keeping our statesmen segregated, immune and mutually detached. This is no mere paradox. Diplomacy is the art of negotiating documents in a ratifiable and therefore dependable form. It is by no means the art of conversation. The affability inseparable from any conversation between Foreign Ministers produces allusiveness, compromises, and high intentions." Quoted in Charles W. Thayer, *Diplomat* (New York: Harper, 1959), p. 109. Also see Harold Nicolson, *Diplomacy* (New York: Oxford University Press, 1964), pp. 52–53.

23. Henry M. Jackson (ed.), *The National Security Council: Jackson Subcommittee Papers on Policy Making at the Presidential Level* (New York: Praeger, 1965), p. 265.

24. Richard F. Pedersen, "National Representation in the United Nations," *International Organization*, XV, No. 2 (Spring 1961), 258.

25. Max Beloff, *New Dimensions in Foreign Policy: A Study in Administrative Experience, 1947–59* (New York: Macmillan, 1961), p. 176. Essay by Chadwick F. Alger in Herbert C. Kelman (ed.), *International Behavior* (New York: Holt, Rinehart and Winston, 1965), p. 265. B. E. Matecki, *Establishment of the International Finance Corporation* (New York: Praeger, 1957), pp. 92, 142–143, 159–160. "Universal, Regional and Bilateral Pattern of International Organization," *State Department Bulletin*, XXII (April 3, 1950), p. 526.

26. Cordier and Foote, *op. cit.*, p. 177.

27. Philip C. Jessup, "Practising Law in the United Nations," speech to the Judicial Conference, Third Judicial Circuit, July 6, 1948.

28. Adlai Stevenson, *Looking Outward*, Robert L. Schiffer and Selma Schiffer (eds.) (New York: Harper and Row, 1961), p. xvii.

29. Arthur J. Goldberg, address before the Association of American Law Schools, December 29, 1966. *Department of State Press Release No. 304*, p. 4. In a post-Middle East crisis speech, the Ambassador pointed out that "acrimonious debate in the UN—deplorable though it may be—does not prevent agreements." On June 6, 1967, the Soviet Union joined in a unanimous resolution for a cease-fire, he added. Six weeks later, the Soviet Union "while still saying harsh words about us in public—joined with us in the search for an acceptable resolution to

conclude the Assembly and provide the general guideline for a peace settlement." (*USUN Press Release* 127, July 27, 1967, p. 3.)

30. See footnote 20, above, for full bibliographical note. The author of Chapter X, pages 163–174, is reliably reported to have been George F. Kennan, although I have not been able to obtain his personal confirmation. Kennan is extraordinarily sensitive about the quest for autonomy: "The truth of the matter is that any great military-occupational government at once takes on certain of the aspects of a sovereign government and is in a position to require that it be treated accordingly, even by the government it purports to represent. Ceasing to be primarily an instrument of policy, it becomes in large measure a policy-making center in its own right." (*Memoirs: 1925–1950* [Boston: Little, Brown, 1967], pp. 371–372.)

31. Samuel P. Huntington has defined an institution as "stable, valued, recurring patterns of behavior." ("Political Development and Political Decay, *World Politics*, XVII [April 1965], p. 394.)

32. Robert Dahl, *Congress and Foreign Policy* (New York: Norton, 1964), pp. 40 ff.

33. Changes in American foreign policy can occur with no trace of UN influence; for example, the disappearance in 1965 of the multilateral force (MLF) idea as a cardinal tenet of United States security policy. In this instance several actors were involved, but not the UN. Someone has said that "the hot line between Washington and Moscow does not pass through U Thant's office." Major bilateral negotiations can take place outside the UN, witness the meetings between Chinese Communist and United States negotiators which have been going on since 1955. Well over two hundred, perhaps even three hundred, such sessions have been held. These negotiations have been described as "the longest established permanent floating diplomatic game in modern history." (Kenneth T. Young, *Diplomacy and Power in Washington–Peking Dealings: 1953–1967* [Chicago: University of Chicago Center for Policy Study, 1967], p. 10.)

34. Walt W. Rostow, "The Great Transition: Tasks of the First and Second Postwar Generations," Sir Montagu Burton lecture, the University of Leeds, England, February 23, 1967, pp. 10–11 of text, obtainable from Mr. Rostow's White House office.

35. Regional intergovernmental organizations are springing up all over the world. "The Yearbook of International Organizations," 1964–1965, lists 150, not including the UN, its specialized agencies, and the three European communities. Not less than 112 have been established since 1945. The 150 are divided as follows geographically: 34 European (East

and West), 28 American, 14 African, three Asian, and 71 "intercontinental" organizations. (Gerard Herberichs, "On Theories of Public Opinion and International Organization," *Public Opinion Quarterly* [Winter 1966–1967], p. 624.)

36. Joseph E. Johnson, "Helping Build New States," in Francis D. Wilcox and H. Field Haviland, Jr. (eds), *The United States and the United Nations* (Baltimore: Johns Hopkins Press, 1961), p. 3.

37. Roger Kahn, *Saturday Evening Post*, January 29, 1966, p. 85. As of May 1968, Goldberg could claim 124 clients.

38. Hedley Bull attacks the "scientific" approach to international relations theory and the "fetish" for measurement. "International Theory: the case for a classical approach," *World Politics* (April 1966), pp. 361–377.

39. In any study of the June 1967 Middle East crisis, an analyst will need to ask an unanswerable question: the role of intelligence in the Israeli decision to blitzkrieg the Arab countries. Jean-Jacques Servan-Schreiber has written that in 1959 the Israelis "deciphered some intelligence information they had acquired during Khrushchev's palace revolution indicating that the Soviet chiefs had never intended to implement their 1956 threat [of atomic war during the Suez attack]. Based on this analysis of what they call the Soviet 'bluff,' the civilian and military leaders in Tel Aviv prepared and carried out their strategy. At no time did they expect Moscow to intervene in the crisis. . . . The Israeli secret services considered the information they had collected in 1959 to be solid." (*L'Exprès*, June 12–18, 1967, translated in *Atlas Magazine* [August 1967], p. 16.) Servan-Schreiber, a highly regarded journalist and publicist, may or may not know what he is talking about. (After all, a Soviet "bluff" in 1956 is not necessarily a harbinger for June 5, 1967.) One must assume that Israel had some information on which to base its final decision. An analyst using the modern technology of political science must make room for the unknown without having the remotest idea if the unknown exists, and if its existence is somehow confirmed, he must determine its relevance to his measurement scale.

40. Ralf Dahrendorf, *Class and Class Conflict in Industrial Society* (Stanford, Calif.: Stanford University Press, reprinted 1966), pp. 112–113. Dahrendorf cites a definition of "meta-theoretical" as "a plausible description of attitudes that guide empirical research without themselves permitting of empirical test."

5/ USUN and How It Functions

The United States Mission to the United Nations "has acquired a corporate personality and an independent reason for existence."[1] The institution described is housed in a fifteen-floor building on the southwest corner of First Avenue and East 45th Street. Directly opposite on the avenue at East River is the General Assembly building and slightly further south, the skyscraper Secretariat building. Until 1961, Mission headquarters were several stories of an office building at Two Park Avenue. Construction of the present headquarters, which cost $3.75 million, was begun in 1959.[2]

The general purposes of a UN mission have been summarized by Ambassador Pedersen, Deputy Representative in the Security Council. The formal reasons are, first, to

72

advise the home government on advantages and disadvantages of using the UN as a diplomatic instrument; second, to establish criteria to determine whether and how specific issues can be raised at the UN; and, third, to evolve methods whereby a government can maximize its gain from UN participation.

The Mission functions in six areas: negotiation and parliamentary action; formulation of policy and tactics; influencing opinion; information-gathering; representation; and public relations. Since the UN is a "permanent conference" with an established agenda, its business "ends" presumably with the disposition of resolutions. This is the negotiation and parliamentary activity.

The least-understood aspect of a mission is the extent of its responsibility in formulating policy and tactics to be followed in the UN. This "internal" role is a government secret, and thus "it is difficult to make any clear estimates of the amount of control delegations have over policies and tactics."[3] Ambassador Pedersen says that while a UN mission may possess a measure of discretion in tactics, it has less influence on policies. Generally, the delegations advise, and nothing more, on policy questions.

The chief instrument in influencing opinion is the UN speech. First, however, there must be a decision as to which opinions are to be persuaded—domestic, foreign, governmental, or private—and to which audience or audiences the speech is to be directed. In most instances, the speech is aimed, first of all, at Assembly committees with the intent of guiding debate in desired directions, discouraging undesirable courses of action, influencing both the negotiation and final vote.[4]

Information-gathering and exchange of information are a time-consuming effort for the delegation, yet extremely important in obtaining a quick reaction to world events before embassies in host countries can prepare and file summaries of such reactions.[5] The representation function speaks for itself.

Public relations is one of the Mission's most important functions since it is more closely watched and covered by the press (and the world press, at that) than most government departments and agencies in Washington. USUN must deal with some three hundred accredited newspaper and other media correspondents. Requests for briefings are continuous. The relationship of the press to the UN and the USUN is one of the most complicated (and unexamined) involvements of American foreign policy. UN correspondents enjoy life in the Glass House, and several have been known to protest bitterly their transfer to other assignments. It is very heady to be close to big names and big events and to be certain that, during international crises, one is writing history. Even more fascinating to some correspondents is the certainty that today's penniless petitioner from some unknown colony before the Trusteeship Council may be tomorrow's Prime Minister or Foreign Secretary.

It is in its press and public relations that the USUN demonstrates another facet of its uniqueness. In a recent study of the UN correspondent, Ronald Rubin[6] has written:

Most reporters have contacts with the U.S. Mission. The United States is involved in most major issues at the United Nations and one looks to the United States and expects it to play a major role at the United Nations.

The responsibilities, he says, of a UN correspondent differ from those of a foreign correspondent "just as diplomacy at the UN differs from diplomacy carried out in foreign capitals."

In contrast to the UN, no foreign capital has the press corps in so centralized a setup. The physical propinquity of the UN operation affords the correspondent a double intimacy unmatched by the organization of the press corps in any foreign capital. The correspondent is more intimate here with both his colleagues and sources than is the case in any other diplomatic venue.

There is a good deal of mail to the USUN and to the Mission Chief from the general public: an average of some two hundred letters daily. This may increase considerably when momentous issues move into UN range or during some dramatic occasions;[7] then it may swell overnight to vast proportions. Yet the writers must all be answered, and they are, usually with one of several form replies.

The permanent USUN staff consists of those persons who serve as representatives in the Assembly, on Assembly committees, the Economic and Social Council (ECOSOC), Trusteeship Council, Security Council, and other UN bodies. The representative and his deputies also represent the United States on the Disarmament Commission, Collective Measures Committee, Peace Observation Commission, Palestine Conciliation Commission, the Committee of Twenty-four, and the Committee on the Peaceful Uses of Outer Space.

Under ECOSOC are seven functional commissions, some of which meet annually, some biennially. The seven United States members of these commissions[8] are paid only during commission sessions unless they are already United States government employees, in which case they serve without further compensation.

The Mission's administrative staff has particular duties which are called "UN Host Country Responsibilities." It administers the specific legal responsibilities of the International Organizations Immunities Act (22 U.S. Code 288).[9]

During a calendar year, approximately thirty different UN bodies will meet in New York for sessions which last from a few days to more than three months. United States delegations to these sessions may range from two officers (in a small body such as the Statistical Commission) to as many as fifty officers during Assembly sessions. Approximately 400 to 450 representatives, advisers, and supporting personnel from the State Department, the Foreign Service, other government agencies, and from

outside the government serve annually on these delegations.[10] The roster of the Delegation to the 21st Session
of the General Assembly totaled 62 persons, starting with
Ambassador Goldberg and down to the last name on the
alphabetical list, Wilbur H. Ziehl, senior adviser, Legal
and International Organization Affairs, United States
Mission to the UN.

Considering the workload of the Mission and the
growth of responsibility owing to the increase of UN
membership from 51 to 124, the annual appropriations
have been quite modest. In the first year, 1946, for only
three months, the appropriation was $240,043. It went
up, naturally, in 1947, to $1,220,478 and more or less
stayed at that figure through 1951. It dropped below $1
million starting in 1952 when the General Services Administration took over the rent, utilities, guard, and cleaning services. It went up over the million-dollar mark in
1959, about when the surge in membership began, and
for the 1966–1967 fiscal year was $1,610,478. Proposed
obligations for fiscal 1967 are $1,631,100, and for fiscal
1968, $1,677,100. Personnel salaries have remained at
about the same ratio, at an average of 83 per cent of the
total appropriation. The remaining 17 per cent has gone
to meet overtime, supplies, equipment, official representation and terminal leave costs, and travel on USUN business. Affiliation fees to the UN and ancillary bodies are
separate appropriations.

Numerical composition of personnel remained fairly

stationary during the tenure of Ambassador Lodge. When he was appointed by President Eisenhower in 1953, there were 180 authorized positions, of which some 25 were employees of the United States Atomic Energy Commission. They had been grafted onto the Mission in 1948 as a result of the Baruch-Lilienthal Report on Atomic Energy.[11] At Lodge's recommendation, these positions were cut out of the Mission budget. In 1954, he lopped off another 40 positions so that 115 remained. When he resigned to run for Vice-President on the Republican ticket with Richard M. Nixon, there were 108 positions, a figure he had maintained from 1956. Since then, the number of positions has risen to 126, a modest enough 17 per cent increase.

Dean Rusk has described taking over in 1947 as director of the Office of International Affairs, which dealt with the UN, and finding on the staff 230 people. He began checking around and discovered that the British Foreign Office had seven people, the Turks but one. So he reduced the staff by a third, to 150, "and I am quite sure that we got more work done because we spent less time reading each other's papers."[12]

As far as USUN appropriations are concerned, the only problem is on the appropriation for entertainment, known in bureaucratese as "representation." Congressional niggardliness is attributed to a malignancy known as "Rooneyism," in tribute to Representative John J. Rooney (D., N.Y.), who cannot understand why a diplomat should drink liquor at the expense of the American taxpayer. Ambassador James J. Wadsworth says that USUN officers must do "a certain amount of modest entertaining for which they can sometimes receive partial reimbursement from the 'representation fund.' " Rooney, chairman of the House Appropriations subcommittee which concerns itself with the State Department budget, calls this "whiskey money."[13]

The delegation advisers consist of two groups: substantive and political (or contact). The latter group is most active during the first weeks of the General Assembly, explaining to other delegates the United States position on which items should be on the UN agenda and in what order. These political advisers, generally Foreign Service officers with particular competence in a geographical area, act as liaison to delegates to whom they are assigned. The substantive advisers come in later when the resolutions are being circulated and negotiated in committees.

The General Assembly delegation has generally included the permanent representative to the UN, as chairman of the delegation (except when the Secretary of State is in attendance); the deputy representative or representatives; two members of Congress, alternating between House and Senate each session, one a Democrat and the other a Republican. Then there are usually six delegates who, as Ambassador Pedersen writes, are selected because they typify "various segments of American life, including inter alia, economic, regional, religious, and racial groups; there is usually at least one woman delegate (traditionally the United States representative on the Human Rights Commission)."[14]

Almost from the beginning of the UN, the custom arose of appointing to Assembly delegations nationally and internationally known personalities—what I would call "noncareer professionals"—as assets in what Ambassador Pedersen has called "the battle for public opinion." He writes:

> *The fact that Dr. Charles Mayo of the Mayo Clinic made the final refutation in the UN of the Soviet Union's charges concerning germ warfare in Korea was certainly instrumental in bringing that particular propaganda campaign to a halt.*[15]

Such an evaluation is highly significant, because to bring into a United States delegation prominent Americans of varying degrees of tact, independence, and experience may have its drawbacks, from the standpoint of correct diplomatic procedure. AFL-CIO President George Meany refused on one occasion to deliver as presented to him the State Department draft of a speech at a UN committee meeting where he was sitting as the United States representative. He suggested that his USUN liaison officer make it instead. Concerned that Meany's refusal would get out among the delegates and cause unfavorable comment, the State Department approved changes suitable to Meany, and he delivered the speech.[16] On the other hand, when this same labor leader rebuts an anti-American polemic by a Communist delegate, the effect is regarded as positively greater than if the same rebuttal had been delivered by a career officer. On another occasion, a United States delegate openly applauded the affirmative majority vote of an Asian-African majority on a colonial question when her delegation decided to abstain. No reprimand was delivered to Mrs. Zelma George, nor, on the other hand, did she resign in protest.

Ambassador Wadsworth has described the process whereby difficulties over instructions are compromised or smoothed over.[17] Although the Assembly delegation is "instructed"—that is, it takes its orders from the State Department—disagreements arise as to instructions. Once or twice a session, he writes, "would be a reasonably accurate estimate as to how often the United States Delegation disagrees strongly enough with the State Department to put the machinery of dissent into motion. When it does feel that strongly, it has a good chance of success."

Various Chiefs of Mission work differently with their delegations, as is to be expected when it is realized that the relationship between them will at most last for a few months of the Assembly session, insufficient time to build up much more than a semiformal acquaintance. Ambassador Goldberg, unlike his predecessors, is a great believer in full-dress regular meetings with the delegation and staff. "Until he introduced this innovation," said one USUN official, "of regular meetings, the right hand didn't know what the left hand was doing; at least now there is some communication around this place."

A meeting schedule is generally circulated at the opening of an Assembly session by the Delegation Secretary. USUN circular No. 46, September 23, 1966, listed these regular meetings:

Counsellor's Meetings with Executive Officers	9:15 A.M. Mondays, Wednesdays, Fridays
The Justice's Meeting with Delegates	9:35 A.M. Mondays, Wednesdays, Fridays
Full Delegation Meeting	9:35 A.M. Tuesdays

These sessions, as will be noted, convene before the usual General Assembly sessions open at 11 A.M. Discussions at these delegation meetings are wide-ranging, frank, and of course confidential.[18]

In the next chapter, I shall deal with the USUN relationship with the Bureau of International Organization Affairs and the relationship between the Assistant Secretary for International Organization Affairs and the Chief of Mission.

Notes

1. Don K. Price, "The New Dimension of Diplomacy," in *The Organization of the U.S. Government for Its New Role in World Affairs* (New York: Woodrow Wilson Foundation, 1951), p. 19. Interestingly, Ernest A. Gross, who served as deputy representative of USUN (1949–1953) has written that "those who make vague appeals for 'support to the United Nations' [are] claiming for it an abstract or corporate existence it does not in fact possess." (*The United Nations: Structure for Peace* [New York: Harper, 1962], p. 8.) Here is an intriguing contrast. Price ascribes to USUN a corporate existence, while

Gross finds that the UN has none, although the raison d'être for USUN is the UN. Actually the UN has as much corporate existence as any tribal tutelary spirit, as any totem where the members "are therefore under a sacred obligation not to kill (destroy) their totem," as Freud has written in *Totem and Taboo* (New York: Moffat, Yard, 1919), pp. 3 ff. Without forcing the analogy too greatly, the totem is hereditary and "is not limited to district or to locality." (I am not quite sure how to analogize with the UN Freud's statement that "members of the same totem are not allowed to enter into sexual relations with each other; that is, that they cannot marry each other.") UN has as much corporate existence as USUN because sovereign states have agreed to transact business transnationally through a central switchboard located in a world center. Of course, other switchboards, hot lines, and arenas exist for bilateral exchanges of messages. Yet it is at the UN that most war crises land as UN agenda items, whether by private Soviet-United States agreement or by some other method. This would indicate that somebody feels that something is to be gained by exploiting the UN. To this extent, the UN has as much corporate existence as, at the very least, A.T.&T.

2. The structure is owned by the General Services Administration, which pays the "rent," utilities, the guard details, and cleaning expenses. The Mission pays for communication costs, furniture, and office equipment. The 126 Mission employees (1966) are paid directly from the USUN budget, but receive no supplemental allowances as normally Embassy employees overseas do. During the annual General Assembly session, delegates, alternates, and advisers are appointed and a dozen or so additional stenographic and secretarial employees are brought into the Mission. Much of the technical data were supplied by Edward Gaumond, Chief Administrative Officer, who is Secretary of the Delegation.

3. Richard F. Pedersen, "National Representation in the United Nations," *International Organization*, XV, No. 2 (Spring 1961), 258. Ambassador Pedersen is an example of how unusual USUN is in the State Department hierarchy. During his long service at the Mission he has gone from a low-ranking post to Ambassador without serving abroad. "The requirement of having people on the spot," a State Department official told me, "who know the ropes at the UN is clear enough but in serving that end, the USUN has developed an institutional strength shared by no other embassy in the Foreign Service nor by the State Department itself."

4. These sentences, being official, really represent the "literary" theory of a mission's behavior. It is really a model, and as a model it is useful for analysis. Under Ambassadors Lodge, Stevenson, and Gold-

berg, the USUN enjoyed varying degrees of leverage on policy. In the case of other UN missions, some ambassadors have great discretion on issues about which their governments have only marginal interest. This discretion is particularly the case with new UN members where the even newer Foreign Offices are inexperienced in international diplomacy or in formulation of instructions. As for discretion in tactics, personal observation has persuaded me that UN missions (except, I suppose, those of the Communist bloc) pretend that when they disagree with their home government it is only on tactics, rarely on policies. UN missions, I have heard it said bitterly, will seek to alter policies, claiming all the while they are exercising a needful flexibility in tactics. Sometimes, at the UN as in other large bodies, tactics are policy. As for the influence of a speech on voting, Ambassador Gross has been quoted: "There's an old saying at the UN that General Assembly debates sometimes change opinions but rarely change votes." (Franz B. Gross [ed.], *The United States and the United Nations* [Norman: University of Oklahoma Press, 1964], p. 86.)

Dag Hammarskjöld felt that "the legislative process in the United Nations is not a substitute for diplomacy. It serves its purpose only when it helps diplomacy to arrive at agreements between the national states concerned. It is diplomacy, not speeches and votes, that continues to have the last word in the process of peace-making." (Address at Ohio State University, *United Nations Review* [March 1958], pp. 10–12.) The UN would make a fine testing ground for Aristide Briand's utterance: "A political speech is not a work of literature. It is an act." According to Ambassador Goldberg, during 1966–1967 he made one hundred speeches at the UN. This figure, of course, is supplemented by oratorical exercises by other USUN delegates to UN bodies. (*USUN Press Release* 127, July 27, 1967, p. 1.)

5. As an example of how the role of USUN has been overlooked by political scientists, I cite the following description about the American President: "No one else has the means to assess on an hour-to-hour basis the outcropping of events in remote places, the quick means of relating a happening in one part of the globe to another 10,000 miles away; no ambassador or military officer is in the continuous contact with foreign leaders everywhere." (Sidney Hyman, "The Art of the Presidency," *Annals of the American Academy*, Vol. 307 [September 1956], p. 8, col. 2.) While the USUN Chief may not have the same world-wide intelligence apparatus as that at the President's disposal nor all his other resources of communication, he can easily be in contact with "foreign leaders" at the UN because the UN is in continuous session and has more embassies and future "embassies" in the form of anticolonial exile

movements attached to itself than any single country, including the United States, could possibly have. In addition, because of Goldberg's close White House relationship, he was allowed to see "all the traffic" which crossed the President's desk.

6. Ronald Rubin, "The UN Correspondent," *Western Political Quarterly*, XVII (December 1964), pp. 615–631.

7. Following publication by the *Saturday Evening Post* of an article which alleged that Adlai Stevenson had acted as a "dove" during the October 1962 missile crisis, the USUN received some five thousand pieces of mail within a week. This is based on authentic but unpublished sources.

8. The seven commissions include: Social, Narcotic Drugs, Status of Women, Statistical, Human Rights, International Commodity, Trade and Population. The Human Rights, Status of Women, and Narcotic Drugs commissions meet annually, the other four biennially.

9. These duties include assistance on visa problems; exemption from real estate, city, and state excise taxes; handling of police problems; hospitality, residential, and office purchase and renting problems; issuance of diplomatic lists for federal, state, and local authorities and business concerns; customs and immigration clearance.

10. Two senior advisers are listed who have never served since their appointment in 1961 by President John F. Kennedy and thereafter by President Johnson. They are AFL-CIO President George Meany and Auto Workers President Walter P. Reuther. Their refusal to serve and the reasons are an indication as to how domestic non-UN problems may sometimes spill over into the Mission. In 1961, Kennedy wanted to appoint Reuther as a representative to the General Assembly as President Eisenhower had appointed Meany and later George Harrison, president of the Brotherhood of Railway Clerks. Meany blocked the appointment of Reuther, with the result that no labor leader was so designated. To compensate for this frustration, Kennedy designated both men as "senior advisers." So far as I know, they have never taken the $93 per diem compensation to which they would be entitled if serving. The information is based on authentic but unpublished sources. Goldberg reinstated the custom of having a U.S. labor leader on the USUN delegation after an eight-year lapse. At the 1967-1968 Session, I. W. Abel, president of the United Steelworkers of America AFL-CIO, served on the delegation by Presidential appointment.

11. USUN headquarters were originally at 250 West 57th Street. Bernard Baruch, named as United States Representative to the UN Atomic Energy Commission, quartered his staff at the Empire State Building. "Correspondents in those days had the impression that Mr.

The "Other" State Department

Baruch had very little to do with the U.S. officers and activities centered on 57th St.," wrote John MacVane in a pamphlet entitled *Embassy Extraordinary: U.S. Mission to the United Nations* (New York: Public Affairs Committee. April 1961), p. 20.

12. Henry M. Jackson (ed.), *The Secretary of State and the Ambassador* (New York: Praeger, 1964), p. 126.

13. James J. Wadsworth, *The Glass House* (New York: Praeger, 1966), p. 177. How important is "representation" is a question which has troubled one State Department Officer. Fisher Howe in "The Computer and Foreign Affairs" (Center for International Systems Research, Occasional Papers, No. 1, Department of State Publication No. 8156, 1966, p. 68), writes: "Is there an orderly way to evaluate the *relative* gains to United States interest of paying attention to certain segments of society, to certain groups, to certain leaders; or to appraise the *relative* merits of different types of approach? No subject is more sedulously avoided. But it cannot be. Money is spent to achieve a purpose. Heretofore refinement of purpose and means in the representational activity has defied all efforts. A computer will not solve this most elusive of problems but its *factoring* capability just might help." (Emphasis in original.)

The greatest portion of the representation allowance goes to the Mission Chief. For fiscal 1966, $17,569 went to Ambassador Goldberg, who with his wife does an enormous amount of entertaining. The next highest amount, $2,978, went to the Deputy Representative. A lowly $136 went for "Administrative Affairs." The requested appropriations for fiscal 1967 and 1968 are for $30,000 each year. Obviously, the USUN must depend on other sources for entertainment of delegates from other missions. I have been told that Goldberg spent $10,000 a year of his own money in addition to the USUN appropriation for his official UN activities.

REPRESENTATION ALLOWANCE FOR USUN, 1947–1966
(based on figures supplied by the Mission)

FISCAL YEAR	AMOUNT	MEMBER NATIONS*	AVERAGE FOR MEMBER
1947	$13,640	56	$243
1956	16,029	79	203
1960	12,878	98	131
1964	28,733	111	259
1966	32,146	120	268

* The averages do not include the United States as a member.

14. Richard F. Pedersen, "National Representation in the United Nations." (*International Organization*, XV, No. 2 [1961], 257.) According to Article 9.2, UN members are allowed five General Assembly representatives. In addition, they may have five alternates, under Rule 21 of the Rules of Procedure. These alternates are not substitutes for the five representatives, but are granted responsibility and authority equivalent to the representatives' plus supporting staff. In effect, the USUN may be said to have ten members during Assembly sessions. As many advisers, experts, and persons of similar status as a member may desire are permitted under Rules 22 and 92. (Alf Ross, *Constitution of the United Nations* [New York: Rinehart, 1950].)

15. Pedersen, *op. cit.*, p. 263.

16. The story is known personally to the writer.

17. Wadsworth, *op. cit.*, p. 179.

18. Delegates and advisers are all subject to the usual FBI security investigation prior to appointment.

6/ The Assistant Secretary of State and the Chief of Mission: Who Rules?

So advanced is computer design that it is today considered quite possible for one of these elaborate electronic brains to have a "nervous breakdown" when faced with some highly complicated problem. There is little question in my mind that a computer with such anthropomorphic ambitions if put to explaining the mysteries of the State Department organization table would collapse in a chaos of clicking sounds and flickering lights.

Let us calmly examine that sector of the State Department which worries about United States representation at the United Nations. In making this examination, we shall see how complicated organizational life becomes when a new subsystem—in this case the United Nations —is introduced into an existing system such as the United States government with all the rigidities of national sovereignty. To begin from the beginning:

January 15, 1944, the Department created the Office of Special Political Affairs to deal with the United Nations-in-being. It was supervised by a special assistant to the Secretary of State. In the organization chart, this office had the technical status of one of the four geographical offices, but no Assistant Secretary of State over it.

January 21, 1948, new name: Office of United Nations Affairs.

October 3, 1949, new name: Bureau of United Nations Affairs. This change in nomenclature also affected the geographic offices, which also became "bureaus." The Hoover Commission's February 1949 report recommended that an Assistant Secretary of State be appointed to run the Bureau of UN Affairs.

August 25, 1954, new name: Bureau of International Organization Affairs with an Assistant Secretary of State for International Organization, I.O., as it is abbreviated.

The Assistant Secretary is one of seven such State Department officers; he has responsibility for instructing United States delegations in international bodies. Specifically, there are five sections within the Bureau concerned with:

1. UN Political and Security Affairs. This office deals with those questions relating to maintenance of international peace and security which come within the purview of Security Council or General Assembly.

2. International Economic and Social Affairs. This office deals with such questions as technical assistance, social and humanitarian and economic issues which come before the GA, ECOSOC, and subsidiary bodies. The director of this office is usually the deputy United States representative to ECOSOC.

3. Dependent Area Affairs. This office handles Trusteeship Council relations. Its director is also the deputy representative to the Council.

4. International Administration. This office handles finance, personnel, organization, and administration of the Mission, the UN Delegation, and delegations to all the UN agencies.

5. International Conferences. This office arranges for United States participation in international meetings. It prepares preliminary delegation lists, obtains travel funds, provides secretarial staffs to assist the Mission. In meetings away from New York, it provides administrative staffs to aid the delegates.

Each of these offices, but particularly, 1, 2, and 3, maintains experts and desk officers who are responsible for drafting position papers on subjects to be discussed at international conferences. A position paper is defined as follows:

1. It includes (*a*) background of a given issue, (*b*) opinions expressed in the past, (*c*) action likely to be taken by other countries.

2. It outlines United States policy and objectives on a given issue.

3. It instructs delegates as to what position to take.

4. It presents fallback positions.[1]

The Bureau officer who prepares the position paper confers (*a*) with the Department's geographical bureaus, each of which maintains advisers on I.O. problems, (*b*) with other sections of the Department, and (*c*) frequently with other agencies in the Executive branch concerned with the particular issue.

To assure policy coordination in areas affecting other Executive departments and agencies, a number of interdepartmental committees exist which presumably meet on regular schedules. One such interdepartmental group, called the UN Economic Committee, comprises representatives from State, Agriculture, Budget Bureau, Commerce, Federal Reserve Board, Council of Economic Advisers, Health-Education-Welfare, Housing and Home Finance, Interior, AID, Labor, and the Treasury. Other interdepartment and interagency committees could be listed, but there is no need. In actual fact, as interviews with responsible officials indicate, these interdepartmental committees are ritualistic, and, as one ranking officer put it, "they are on the lowest conceivable level."

"These committees meet once or twice a year," he said. "If there's an important issue, an ad hoc meeting is called by I.O. with the top people involved and they thrash it out. The standing group is meaningless. You need a specific committee to deal with a specific problem."

On paper, these committees have State Department officers as chairmen and secretaries, usually seconded from the I.O. Bureau. Practically, these committees which look so impressive on the organization chart have no substantive assignment. However, the Bureau itself, even though it is said to be the least prestigious within the Department, has a rather imposing work load. This is owing to the extraordinary number of international conferences in which the United States participates. In 1962, for example, the Government sent out working delegations to new international conferences at the rate of *one a day*. Of the 2,786 persons who represented the United States at these conclaves, 1,117 were State or Foreign Service officers, 1,232 were from other government departments, 57 were from Congress, 380 were from the public.[2]

What seems to be quite clear is that the I.O. Bureau's relationship to the USUN depends largely on the relationship between the Assistant Secretary and the Mission Chief. That relationship, in turn, depends on the personality and ambitions of the Mission Chief. During the chieftaincy of Adlai Stevenson, Assistant Secretary Harlan Cleveland, a political appointee, but, equally important, a "noncareer professional," was a dominant figure at the Mission. In the case of Justice Goldberg, there is little doubt that Joseph Sisco, an able Foreign Service career official, was Goldberg's deputy.[3] This superordination of the USUN over the I.O. Bureau, as is presently the case (1968), means that the USUN has returned to those golden days when Henry Cabot Lodge ruled the roost and even Secretary of State Dulles could do little about it, as we shall see later.

Even an observer sympathetic to the I.O. Bureau has conceded:

The International Organization Bureau is above all a servant of policy directives not its own and yet must find ways of effectuating these in a diplomatic setting that includes virtually all the nations of the world. The multiplicity of subject matter combines with this function of internal brokerage to yield a complicated and sometimes unwieldy task within the United States Government of conferences, negotiations, compromise and other intrafamilial dealings.[4]

This is putting it mildly, because the situation of the Assistant Secretary is more difficult than Bloomfield describes it. "In the policy-making echelons of the U.S. Government, the key figure regarding U.N. participation is the Assistant Secretary of State for International Organization Affairs," he writes.[5] The phrase "key figure" is

93

ambiguous and surely unquantifiable. On the next two pages, Bloomfield adds:

> *Protocol places a handicap on the Assistant Secretary of State in carrying out his duties. The U.S. Representative, particularly when he sits as a member of the President's Cabinet, outranks the Assistant Secretary through whom he normally receives his instructions. . . . In the New York setting . . . the Assistant Secretary tends to remain far more of a background figure vis-à-vis the mission chief.*

Not until 1960 was the Assistant Secretary made a full representative on the General Assembly delegation. It is difficult to see how, in the face of such a catalogue of disabilities, the Assistant Secretary is "the key figure regarding U.N. participation."

The fact is that he is not the key figure. Or, he can be the key figure if and only if the USUN Chief permits him to act, as Stevenson permitted Assistant Secretary Harlan Cleveland and Deputy Assistant Secretary Richard N. Gardner. Cleveland and Gardner were not State Department career-oriented. In addition, Cleveland had White House access, which the present Assistant Secretary lacks. What could be said about the Stevenson-Cleveland period is that the I.O. Bureau took over USUN functions, something which Ambassador Lodge would not have countenanced.

However, it is also true that when Ambassador Stevenson disagreed with the State Department's handling of the Article 19 arrearages issue, he acted in such a fashion as to reverse overnight the Department's policy.[6] One can propound this theory: USUN power is residual and monopolistic. It can be shared with the Assistant Secretary and the I.O. Bureau, but the decision to share is for the USUN Chief to make. And when goal congruence between USUN and State Department is lacking, the USUN Chief may act in such a fashion as to commit the Government to positions which neither "the key figure" nor the Secretary of State himself intended. Since the USUN Chief is generally an imposing national figure with political resources or White House friendships, it is hard to envision reprisals being visited on him by his nominal superiors as if he were a United States Consul in some corner of a foreign field. Less and less are United States ambassadors political appointees. But the USUN Chief, since the Senator Austin designation, has been a political appointee and, in each case, with a demonstrated interest in foreign affairs and the UN. Thus the USUN Chief has bargaining power which no career official, bound by hierarchical ties, possesses. So long as the President needs the USUN Chief, the USUN Chief does not need the State Department or the I.O. Bureau.[7]

Let me be clear. I am not suggesting that the USUN Chief is a runaway delinquent of some kind, defying authority for the sheer pleasure of it. A man who has spent his life in politics, or in the labor movement, or on the highest court in the land, or as a governor or senator is a man with rather forceful ideas of his own. In large part, this very combination of background, intellect, and personality determined the President to appoint him our chief spokesman at the UN. It is, therefore, highly unlikely that such a person is going to accept "instructions" in as complex an environment as the UN without a murmur. If a USUN noncareer professional has particularly acerbic views about colonialism—views which may be uncongenial to the State Department—it is quite possible that such a man will not easily accept instructions to support positions which Asian and African members would regard as procolonial.

Second, I am not suggesting that the USUN Chief is one of nature's noblemen because he may defy State Department policy. I am suggesting that in public appreciation USUN ranks high because of the quality and public standing of the men who have run the Mission, because they are part of the President's official and unofficial family (at least in the case of Lodge and Goldberg), and because they share the limelight with him to a greater degree than statutory Cabinet members.

Third, so long as the Assistant Secretary for I.O. is a Foreign Service career officer and the USUN Chief is not, the USUN Chief will have no difficulty, if he wishes, in being a first among equals.[8]

Fourth, while the I.O. Bureau was undergoing name changes, hoping to have its status upgraded, the USUN was more and more becoming, with Presidential backing, an institution with its own identity.[9]

Fifth, the I.O. and the Assistant Secretary have their

problems not only with USUN but also with their own colleagues in Washington. Assistant Secretary Francis O. Wilcox (now dean of the School of Advanced International Studies, Johns Hopkins University) and his deputy "often had rough going in persuading their high level colleagues (in Washington) to include the UN as a major element in foreign policy formation."[10] Such conflicts arise because the same events or challenges to American policies can evoke different responses in USUN, in the State Department, or among different bureaus within the Department itself. The responses may differ as to tactics or strategy because USUN, as part of the UN, and some State Department bureaus are more issue-oriented than is the State Department itself. In one situation the USUN Chief altered a high-level decision, which an issue-oriented bureau within the Department had been unable to do on its own. This still unpublicized case concerns authorization by the Department of Commerce in Fall 1965 of the sale of six single-engine Cessna aircraft to the Republic of South Africa. The African desk of the State Department objected on grounds that consummation of the sale would violate the UN arms embargo against Pretoria. Higher officials in the State Department ignored the protest on the grounds that the planes were unarmed and therefore were in a gray area. (An additional factor was that Senator Bourke B. Hickenlooper, a member of the Africa subcommittee of the Foreign Relations Committee, was urging approval of the sale.)

Deputy Assistant Secretary J. Wayne Fredericks in the Department's African Affairs section (and now a Ford Foundation executive) telephoned Justice Goldberg at the USUN and alerted him to the proposed airplane sale. Goldberg promptly called the then Undersecretary of State Thomas C. Mann and asked that the sale be canceled. Goldberg based his protest on the argument that a few planes were not worth certain injury to American influence at the UN. The sale was canceled.[11]

More recently, Goldberg undertook on his own initiative to raise the serious question of Soviet persecution of dissident intellectuals. As I have pieced the story together, sometime late in February 1968 he decided the time had come not only to reply to the unending Soviet propaganda attacks in the UN Commission on Human Rights but, further, to counterattack the Kremlin for its disregard of the basic freedoms envisioned under the Charter. He was "sick and tired of listening to these wild Soviet charges against America and not fighting back."

He thereupon wrote himself a set of formal instructions which he asked Assistant Secretary Sisco to transmit back to him at USUN. These instructions ordered a speech to be prepared detailing Soviet persecutions but with the proviso that it should not be "a cold war speech." Rather it should reflect Goldberg's "fidelity to the Universal Declaration of Human Rights setting forth principles to which you have been committed for a lifetime."

Work began on the speech on March 5 at the USUN offices in New York with a request to State Department researchers to supply any material they might have on Soviet moves against intellectual freedom but with no indication to them as to what the material was for. The speech was prepared during the next morning and during a staff conference luncheon presided over by Goldberg, where it was read aloud and approved by Goldberg paragraph by paragraph. At 3:30 the speech began to be typed and then retyped with corrections. Goldberg was scheduled to speak at 5 P.M. at the Commission session; the text was finally ready a few minutes before the hour for Goldberg to carry across First Avenue from Mission headquarters to the UN conference room.

In the meantime UN correspondents had been alerted that Goldberg would have something newsworthy to say in person at the Commission at 5 P.M. The "in person" was important since the official United States representative to the Human Rights Commission, Morris B. Abram, would normally have made such a declaration. Goldberg's presence lent the occasion high political significance.

A few minutes after 5 P.M. Goldberg began. He quoted as his authorities and sources only those criticisms and protests against Moscow's mistreatment of its intellectuals that had been made publicly by Soviet citizens and foreign Communist leaders. The speech caught the Soviet delegation completely off guard and their replies were more *tu quoque* than usual. A large amount of public attention in the form of news stories and favorable mail followed, according to Mission sources.

The next morning, Goldberg's speech was criticized by

a high State Department official at a staff conference on
the grounds that it would disturb Soviet-United States
"bridge-building" policies. Assistant Secretary Sisco de-
fended the speech against a colleague who outranked him,
as well as—at least on the organization chart—Goldberg.
Quite clearly, senior State Department officials, with
policy-initiating prerogatives, were unaware that Goldberg
was going to speak on a subject of great sensitivity to the
Soviet Union and, therefore, of equal sensitivity to those
State Department officials dealing with Moscow.

Despite the rebuke, nothing happened to Goldberg. It
can be assumed that his speech—so far as can be judged,
it has neither upset nor strengthened understanding between the countries—did not, however, meet with White
House disapproval.

The conflict between the State Department bureau
and USUN would seem unresolvable because more and
more it is difficult for the USUN and its staff to separate
its operations in the field of diplomacy from its inevitable
intrusion into policy-making. The ordinary United States
diplomatic mission is expected to fulfill a role which has
been defined as follows:

> *Precisely and quite simply, the professional service ren-*
> *dered by the diplomat is* the minimizing of distortion and
> friction in cross-cultural communications and operations. . . .
> *In rendering this service the diplomat finds himself operating*
> between *cultures and sometimes in the midst of several*
> *simultaneously.* [*Emphasis in original.*][12]

This description of the "new diplomacy" describes USUN operations rather well, and particularly the assets of men like Adlai Stevenson or Justice Goldberg. "The role of policy making," writes Rossow, "is by definition that of political leadership."[13] If political leadership is an empirical fact—as in the case of a twice Democratic candidate for President or a former Cabinet member who went to the Supreme Court—can policy-making be far behind? And if the Ambassador is, like Ball, a former Undersecretary of State—the Department's Number Two man—are there many State Department officials prepared to oppose him regarding policy differences?[14]

The fact that the USUN has a public figure at its head makes it easy to personalize the Mission. It is rare that an American embassy can claim reification of its chief actor, assuming such a state would be desirable. The press rarely exhibits any particular interest in whether a United States ambassador agrees or disagrees with United States foreign policy. It is assumed that the American ambassador agrees or else he does not disagree sufficiently to resign or seek transfer from his overseas post. The USUN Chief's reification makes him a target for media speculation: is Justice Goldberg a dove, a hawk, or both? Did Adlai Stevenson agree or disagree with the Bay of Pigs invasion? Why did Goldberg resign?[15] The speculation may be wildly incorrect, but the very fact that stories are written about the USUN as an actor with its own subsystem would indicate why the role of the Assistant Secretary of State for I.O. affairs is so limited within the combined UN-USUN subsystems. Even though Justice Goldberg had a more intimate relation with the White House than Adlai Stevenson ever did, nevertheless, their problems and views are news because of the forum in which they are involved.[16]

Perhaps one might conclude this chapter by recalling Woodrow Wilson's famous phrase that the President of the United States is free to be "as big a man as he can." Within limits, so is the USUN Chief, particularly in the case of Adlai Stevenson or Ambassador Lodge, an aspirant to the Presidency during his USUN incumbency. At critical moments in the nation's diplomacy, the USUN Chief becomes its immediate, visible, tangible embodiment. When the third Arab-Israeli war broke out June 5, 1967, the shape of the American response was swiftly apparent because of the UN and the voice of the USUN Chief. Arab spokesmen at the Security Council charged that American planes had bombed Arab military positions. Within minutes and in full view of nationwide television, the United States reacted through the voice of the USUN Chief. It is the necessity of instantaneous response and the continuity of response in this theatrically dramatic form—whether Malik versus Gross, Sobolev versus Lodge, Zorin versus Stevenson, or Fedorenko versus Goldberg—which has made the UN and USUN so strikingly unavoidable and therefore indispensable in the schema of American foreign policy. This US-

USUN atmosphere creates different values or a different ordering of values—and, therefore, commitments—in USUN. These commitments may be accommodated by the State Department but may also interfere with its objectives, or at least tactics.

Notes

1. "Focus on the US in the UN," *Intercom*, IV (New York: Foreign Policy Association, May–June 1962), pp. 19–29.

2. U.S. Department of State Publication No. 7548, I.O. & Conference Series 40, released June 1963, p. 3.

3. Lodge's biographer describes how "Joseph Sisco, a State Department career man, flew up to Beverly [Mass.] one Saturday [1957] with the department's draft of its position [on disarmament]. Lodge turned an old journalist's eye on its impenetrable bafflegab. 'I don't understand it,' he told Sisco. 'If I don't understand it, how in the world can we expect the U.N. to understand it? Let's see if we can't express our position in a nutshell.' Lodge tried to boil it all down to one paragraph. The two worked over the wording." (William J. Miller, *Henry Cabot Lodge* [New York: James H. Heineman, Inc., 1967], pp. 281–282.)

4. Lincoln Bloomfield, *The United Nations and U.S. Foreign Policy* (Boston: Little, Brown, 1960), p. 15.

5. *Ibid.*, p. 261.

6. I shall discuss this case in detail in Chapter 8.

7. There is some historical precedent for this problem. Duff Cooper, in his biography *Talleyrand*, writes: "Talleyrand was not a convenient Ambassador from the point of view of the Government that he represented. An Ambassador should be, in fact as in theory, the subordinate of his Minister for Foreign Affairs. When the Ambassador is a bigger man than the Minister the instrument becomes top heavy. Not only was Talleyrand a far more important person in the eyes of the world than any of Louis-Philippe's Ministers, but he also had his own particular methods of conducting business that were neither in accordance

with diplomatic usage nor with democratic ideas." (New York: Harper, 1932), p. 325.

8. The regional Assistant Secretaries, of course, have far more power: "He's the first person on the ladder who can *commit* the United States of America," Paul H. Nitze is quoted as having said. (Roger Hilsman, *To Move a Nation* [New York: Doubleday, 1967], p. 29.) In fact there has been in recent years a general deterioration of influence among Assistant Secretaries of State, regional, liaison, or administrative. Little prestige attaches to these positions today.

9. Robert D. Murphy, *Diplomat among Warriors* (New York: Doubleday, 1964), p. 365. The former State Department official describes the state of Bureau morale, when he took over in 1953, as low because the McCarthy investigations into the State Department "had been concentrated on people assigned to the office of UN affairs." He adds: "While the office of UN Affairs at the State Department was thus being half-smothered under a cloud of innuendo, the American delegation at UN headquarters was flourishing. Aware of Roosevelt's high hopes for the world organization, Truman decided in 1945 to enhance the status of the American Ambassador to the UN by informally ranking that official practically as a member of the President's Cabinet, and he appointed to that post Warren R. Austin, a statesman of great dignity and charm who had been senator from Vermont, for 14 years. This selection by the Democratic President of a Republican Ambassador was indicative of the intent to lift United States policy at the UN indisputably above domestic politics."

10. Joseph P. Lash, *Dag Hammarskjold* (New York: Doubleday, 1961).

11. This story is based on personal knowledge.

12. Robert Rossow, "The Professionalization of the New Diplomacy," *World Politics*, No. 4 (July 1962), p. 563.

13. *Ibid.*, p. 564.

14. "Mr. Ball, as UN Ambassador will you regard yourself as the lawyer for the Administration or a participant in policy-making?" asked Pauline Frederick, NBC correspondent at the UN. Ball replied:

"Both. Both. As a high official of the United States government I will feel a very definite obligation to urge my views on the President, the Secretary of State, and the Administration. I'm sure this is one of the reasons why the President asked me to serve, because he knows my views, he's listened to them in the past; he has always given me my day in court, and I am sure he will now." ("Meet the Press" Transcript [May 5, 1968], p. 13, National Broadcasting Corp. mimeo).

Or, one could say, same Goldberg melody, different words.

15. In December 1967, a spate of stories were published in the American and world press about the imminence of Goldberg's resignation as USUN Chief. Where the stories originated was difficult to say, although there was some possibility that a few White House officials, unfriendly to Goldberg, were circulating the resignation reports alleging that he was a "dove" on American policy in Vietnam. Regardless of the source of the stories or their accuracy at the time, their prominence in the domestic and world press was noteworthy. (The resignation of HEW Secretary John Gardner, a key Cabinet post, during this period hardly excited as much public discussion as the *possible* resignation of Goldberg.) Even more interesting was speculation as to whether Goldberg was or was not in total sympathy with President Johnson's policies on Vietnam. Goldberg finally did resign April 25, 1968 but stayed on, at the President's request, until June 1968.

16. Robert Dahl, *Modern Political Analysis*, (Englewood Cliffs, N.J.: Prentice-Hall, 1963), p. 11. "In many [political] systems, roles remain the same even when played by a succession of individuals."

7/ Henry Cabot Lodge, 1953–1960

Whenever an aide carried the tidings to USUN Chief Henry Cabot Lodge that "the (State) Department wants us to do this," Lodge reportedly would explode: "Who in the Department is telling me I can't do something that the President of the United States has ordered me to do? Tell me, who said so?"[1]

Unquestionably, Lodge made the USUN the power it is today; or, at least, he gave it such a head start that, short of a Presidential decree, there is no way it can be reduced to the level of an embassy. In fact, the USUN may well be described as the embassy that never was.

Robert D. Murphy, in his autobiography, tells of an incident which took place shortly after he became Assistant Secretary for International Organization Affairs.[2] He and his colleagues at the office of UN affairs in Washington had decided that the United States vote on a resolution during the Korean debate should be "Yes." Secretary Dulles approved the decision. Instructions went off to USUN to vote "Yes" the next day. The next day, Murphy read in the newspaper that Lodge had voted "No." When he remonstrated with Lodge over the telephone about failure to follow instructions, he was told: "Instructions? I am not bound by instructions from the State Department. I am a member of the President's Cabinet and accept instructions only from him." When Murphy protested that "you are head of an embassy and our ambassadors take instructions from the Secretary of State," Lodge replied, "I take note of the Department's opinions." Murphy said he would discuss the matter with Secretary Dulles. To this, Lodge responded, "Yes, do that; he will set you straight." Murphy writes:

> When I did report to Dulles, he listened carefully without comment until I finished, and then said: "This is one of those awkward situations which require special consideration. If it happens again, just tell me and I'll take care of it."

For an ambassador to disagree with his "home office" is not unusual.[3] To do so consistently, even when the disagreement is with the Secretary of State himself, is rather unusual. The Lodge view of USUN was that its virtual autonomy within the State Department was unchallengeable, says Murphy, adding that Lodge "would tolerate no poaching on what he considered his own preserve."[4]

Another example of Lodge's independence on an issue of some gravity—the 1956 Suez crisis—is reported by former United States Ambassador to the United Kingdom Winthrop W. Aldrich.[5] He recounts that Murphy, then Undersecretary of State, called by transatlantic phone to tell him, Lord Salisbury, Harold Macmillan, and R. A. Butler that the State Department had instructed Ambassador Lodge to vote the next day at the UN in favor of a Belgian amendment concerning withdrawal of troops from Suez. If the amendment were to fail of adoption, he was to abstain on an African-Asian resolution. Instead of following these instructions, Lodge abstained on the Belgian amendment, and when it was defeated, he voted for the African-Asian resolution.

In other words [writes Aldrich] the action taken by the United States Delegation to the United Nations was diametrically opposite to the instructions which I had been informed Lodge had received from the State Department. . . . The State Department was not responsible for the action taken by Lodge on November 23. . . . I have never been able to find out how the reversal actually occurred. Of course, President Eisenhower himself may have authorized Lodge's action.

On April 5, 1967, I interviewed Robert D. Murphy and asked him about the Aldrich article.[6] He told me that "Ambassador Lodge did exceed his instructions." In other words, there is no record to show that President Eisenhower did indeed authorize the United States representative to reverse his instructions. In his interview, Murphy told me:

> Cabot had the advantage of having strong pull with Ike because Ike was grateful to him for his work in the 1952 campaign. Cabot felt he was stronger than Dulles, and Dulles was determined not to get into the same scrape with his President that his uncle, Robert Lansing, another Secretary of State, had gotten into with Woodrow Wilson.[7]
>
> Cabot had some good points, like the idea of an immediate riposte to the Communists instead of waiting. He was impulsive and was fond of his autonomy and presented Dulles with a real problem. Dulles didn't trust Lodge to follow instructions, so he came to New York during the critical time of Hungary and Suez. Lodge, of course, had his eye on the White House.[8]

Murphy emphasized that "only a strong Secretary of State can stymie an ambassador at the United Nations. If Dulles had been strong with the White House he could have stopped Lodge."[9]

The Lodge argument that things happen too fast at the UN, thereby necessitating independence for USUN, is one that finds supporters and critics. Max Beloff writes that

> in multilateral negotiations the national interest cannot be settled in advance, but is worked out cooperatively in a "seminar" atmosphere, more like that of any interdepartmental committee. One of the features of the new type of multilateral negotiation is that one can never be certain what is

going to come up next. This makes detailed instructions on tactics impossible.¹⁰ [*Emphasis added.*]

On the other hand, a USUN official who has been more observer than participant disagreed with the argument. He said:

> *In multilateral meetings you can always ask for instructions or push for an adjournment. Surprise moves in the UN context are meaningless. Pulling a fast one on a Big Power is not of much value and not a victory even though there may be a momentary advantage.*

Ernest A. Gross, who served as USUN deputy representative from November 1949 to March 1953 and was often acting representative because of Senator Warren Austin's illness, has offered evidence on both sides of the argument.¹¹ In January 1950, while the Security Council was discussing a Disarmament Commission report, Soviet Ambassador Jacob Malik suddenly rose from his seat at the Council table and walked out on the grounds that "Kuomintang clique" presence instead of Communist China meant that the Council was illegally composed. Therefore, the USSR could no longer participate. Thus began the famous Soviet walkout from the Council. Ambassador Gross recalls:

> *We had no instructions to take because we didn't know what was going to happen. It was an illustration of how sometimes you have to do things in an impromptu manner without guidance from one's betters and hoping that it's the right thing to do. . . . But it seemed obvious at the time, so I asked*

for the floor immediately. I made a little statement in which I said that it seemed to me there was no reason why the Security Council shouldn't carry on with its business and proceed to the subject at hand, a very brief, not argumentative statement.

He adds, "You don't always need instructions; a delegate can know the policy and how to vote without instructions."[12]

Ambassador Gross, it would appear, disposes of the things-happening-too-fast evidence by pointing out that the American delegation

had the great advantage of having the telephone at our beck and call unlike the Europeans or other delegates. We could always leave a Security Council meeting while the consecutive translation was going on and call Washington and report what was going on. . . . It's the actual reason for the consecutive translation system in the Security Council, to give the delegates the opportunity to confer. In our case we had the double advantage of having the opportunity to confer with other delegates and when necessary with the command post in Washington.[13]

What would seem clear from the foregoing discussion is that Ambassador Lodge simply was not going to be bothered by the State Department unless Secretary Dulles was physically present at the UN to supersede him.

Dean Andrew Cordier of Columbia University's School of International Affairs confirmed in an interview with me that the Dulles-Lodge relationship was so poor that Dag Hammarskjöld was frequently the go-between in UN affairs.[14] This was always with Ambassador Lodge's full approval. As Cordier said, "The direct contact between Hammarskjöld and Dulles was desirable, particularly if Lodge couldn't persuade Dulles." He gave as an example the case of the American fliers who were held prisoner after the Korean war was over. While Secretary-General Hammarskjöld was trying to persuade the Chinese to release the pilots, "Dulles was issuing condemnatory statements."

Even the White House [said Cordier] was seeking some way to restrain Dulles to speak less publicly. Lodge couldn't deal with Dulles, so Hammarskjöld, with Lodge's advice, telephoned Dulles to emphasize the need for restraint by all sides. Why couldn't the White House have just told Dulles to exercise restraint? Because Dulles was so much the Secretary of State as hadn't been the case in the previous administration.

Another example of this Lodge-Hammarskjöld-Dulles[15] relationship occurred sometime between the end of October and early November 1956, during the Suez crisis. Ambassador Lodge could not "get across" to Dulles the Hammarskjöld reason for wanting United Nations Emergency Forces (UNEF) on Egyptian soil. With Ambassador Lodge's full agreement, the Secretary-General phoned Dulles in Washington to explain what the UN had done with UNEF to make sure that the United States government knew what the Secretary-General was doing.[16]

The USUN's upstream struggle for increased bargaining power with other actors in the foreign policy-making system did not begin with Ambassador Lodge. It may well have begun under Senator Austin, our first official USUN Chief.[17] In 1952, it was reported that "America's representative to the United Nations and its specialized agencies are furthermore to some degree independent of any central United States direction and discipline." This independence had a threefold origin, said the report:

1. "Deficiencies and obscurities within the government as a whole."

2. The need to "adjust to the necessary 'politics' for gaining support for our basic policies in the United Nations."

3. The need to gain congressional support.[18]

The UN Charter formally describes six organs: Security Council, General Assembly, Economic and Social Council, Trusteeship Council, International Court of Justice, the Secretariat.[19] As one observes the USUN in its day-to-day operations one is tempted to suggest that the USUN is well on its way to becoming a "seventh" organ as it seeks exclusive regulation or management of UN relationships.

In large measure this is due to the great accessibility to the President which Goldberg enjoyed and a special definition of his status which never was so precisely described by any President before Johnson. President Johnson said that "each President has reflected the faith and the firmness of our commitment to the United Nations by always calling upon distinguished citizens of very high achievement to serve in this honored office."[20] He then went on to refer to Goldberg thus: (1) as "an old and trusted friend of mine"; (2) as "a counselor of many years"; (3) "He will sit in our Cabinet"; (4) "He will always have direct and ready access to, and the full and respectful confidence of, the President of the United States and the Secretary of State"; (5) "In his new office, he will speak not only for an administration, but will speak for an entire nation."

These are five very important roles for one man in his relation to a Chief Executive—friend, adviser, Cabinet member, confidant, administration and national spokesman. Rhetoric, of course; but also definable resources which are not in the possession of many other American government officials. Admittedly, what is offered here is a job description, not a definition of a multifaceted role which can easily be tested. Furthermore, it may be asked, what happens to the total description if one of the attributes accorded by the President is withdrawn? Obviously on the day that Johnson no longer regards Ambassador Goldberg as a friend, the other roles will become nominal and formal. Or supposing, while remaining friend, Goldberg cannot get the President's ear as he could not on the Vietnam issue, what meaning do the other four aspects of the job have? Are these roles dominoes subject to "domino theory"?

As stated earlier, "accessibility" is not necessarily influence. To have the sovereign's tilted ear is important if he is willing to listen. Goldberg enjoyed great tactical freedom at the UN and was permitted to plan his own tactics with little or no consultation either at White House or Secretary of State level. By Presidential order, from the outset of his embassy he had the right to see "all the traffic," meaning all cables and reports, no matter how secret, which came across the President's desk. He had the right to call the secretary of the State Department, a little-publicized figure who keeps copies of the most confidential, "eyes only" messages to the Secretary of State, and ask to see these messages, or have them read to him over a secret telephone. He could disagree with the Secretary of State and often did, particularly on Vietnam policy. He could get the President on the phone at any time he thought necessary—but on certain issues, notably Vietnam, all this accessibility meant little so far as influence is concerned. While he had large-scale influence on Middle East policy and Cyprus, and to a lesser extent on South Africa where he pushed a policy of what he has called "visible disengagement," he was unsuccessful in persuading either the President or the State Department to accept, for example, Warsaw or Bucharest as the seat of preliminary negotiations with Hanoi.

In this view, Goldberg really sought to act beyond his competence—Vietnam was not ever really UN business—and admittedly failed because at some point his resources ran out. Clearly no sovereign wants his negotiator to be too independent, too desirous of authority, too infractious, too argumentative. That is undoubtedly the reason why Johnson selected as his negotiators with Hanoi Averell Harriman and Cyrus Vance, who would accept Presidential orders without demurring. These appointments were made by a President who has openly praised Goldberg as a great negotiator. It is undoubtedly true that being excluded from the preliminary stages of the Hanoi-Washington contacts deeply disappointed Goldberg.

The point of this long aside is that a USUN chief who seeks autonomy and demands a dominant role in *all* foreign policy decision-making may find his efforts counter-productive at crucial moments in the sovereign-ambassadorial relations at USUN. He may have many achievements to his credit in skewing American foreign policy in a direction congruent with his own views but when the sovereign speaks, no USUN Chief can do a thing about it except get out as gracefully as possible or wait for another opportunity. By Spring 1967, Goldberg had tired of waiting.

Obviously the USUN Chief role vis-à-vis the sovereign can change if the sovereign decides to downgrade the UN as an actor in American foreign policy or to upgrade the UN. For example, Clayton Fritchey, newspaper columnist and Ambassador Stevenson's public affairs officer, has written:

Goldberg obviously has the ear of the President, but what he says on the vital issues, such as Vietnam and Chinese

*representation, apparently goes in one ear and out the other.
Johnson seems willing to coddle his U.N. representative, even
let him make pro-peace speeches, as long as they don't go too
far, but that's about it.*[21]

Fritchey offers no evidence to support this argument,
although it is known that Goldberg regarded his influence
on United States policy in Vietnam as minor. On the
China issue, however, Goldberg convened a background
press briefing for American correspondents in his private
conference room in early 1967. There he discussed the
matter with a frankness about his own position and the
State Department's which belies Fritchey's statement.
Perhaps, the explanation for the misunderstanding about
Goldberg is expressed elsewhere in the article. Fritchey
writes:

*Men as famous as Stevenson, Lodge, and Goldberg, have
large public followings of their own; their views on almost all
issues they have to deal with at the U.N. are already widely
known; such men are sometimes better known than the
Secretary of State;* their very appointment arouses expectations of certain policies being carried out. [*Emphasis added.*][22]

I shall deal with the Goldberg role in greater detail in
Chapter 10, particularly since the close links between the
USUN and the I.O. Bureau (which did not exist during
the Lodge incumbency) make it possible to argue that in
UN matters, the I.O. Bureau has become part of the
USUN subsystem, while technically it remains part of the
State Department subsystem.[23]

This theme is only speculation because the putative

absorption of the I.O. Bureau by the USUN is much too recent to allow of empirical examination. It is only an idea advanced by competent observers within and without the foreign policy establishment, one of whom told me, "[Joseph] Sisco sneezes when [Ambassador] Goldberg takes snuff."

This theme should be examined within the following five-part hypothesis:

1. As the United States has, with the growth of UN membership, lost its automatic majority and perhaps even its so-called "blocking third," there is a greater need for energy input to ensure United States influence on UN policy, the reciprocal output.

2. This energy input depends to a great extent on the quality and leadership of the USUN and its Chief.

3. Dependence on an external institution like the UN for legitimating United States foreign policy means an increase in USUN resources and bargaining power vis-à-vis the State Department.

4. This increase in resources and bargaining power, by logical extension, will lead to greater and greater influence on foreign policy by USUN relative to the State Department.

5. The I.O. Bureau will handle then the flow of routine policy-making decisions, but on important policy questions, like Vietnam or Southwest Africa, USUN decision-influencing powers can reach a level of equality with State, subject to the willingness of the President to tolerate such a state of affairs, as for example President Tru-

man did for so long in the case of General Douglas MacArthur during the Korean war, or as President Eisenhower did in the case of Secretary of the Treasury George Humphrey's attack on the proposed federal budget in January 1957.[24]

These views fly counter to those of former Deputy Assistant Secretary of State for International Organization Affairs Richard N. Gardner, who has written:

U.S. foreign policy is not made by the United Nations, nor is U.S. foreign policy made by the United States Mission to the United Nations. The center of decision on U.N. affairs, as on all other matters of our foreign policy is Washington, D.C.[25]

Gardner's statement, written in 1963, ignores the possibility that the USUN Chief always has the power to change policy in a specific direction, *if he chooses to act*. This is because the USUN chieftaincy has become a bigger and bigger position in the hierarchical structure of government policy process.

From the standpoint of systems analysis, such a view may be irrelevant since it is pursuit of "black-and-white" superordination in State-USUN relations. Even further, such a view may be seen as signaling a failure to regard the USUN and State as actors in a subsystem with a fairly large cast of influential actors using their differential resources in bargaining with each other over a wide range of specific issues.[26]

Yet in real life, whether baseball or congressional roll calls, there is a scorecard by which certain empirical judgments are made, such as who or what won. Real life consists in determining winners at the end of contests—even winners temporarily on issues evanescent. To test a theory of super- or subordination in a policy process is not to invalidate the subsystem approach. An actor, A, with greater bargaining power than another actor, B, is ahead of the game at a moment of decision. A is the winner in a black-and-white game or in a black-and-white inning; A is the winner because A won or A told B what to do or A made B do something he would not otherwise have done.

Of course, the bargaining process may lead to a "no-win" outcome. Two chess players may take a draw because their "bargaining power" is visibly equal. Therefore we can say neither player in that given general setting had "bargaining power" because the concept of bargaining presupposes some resolution of a conflict, and when you draw in chess, you either start another game or go home. Yet the example of a chess match is not truly relevant because we are dealing with but two actors (although the quasi-infinity of moves and permutations is part of the act) as against a wide variety of actors in a political subsystem. And most important, there is an intangible attribute to the policy process: men's motivations, their interpretations of events, or their legal courses of action based on normative stands.

In analyzing the USUN-UN-State Department relationship, we cannot avoid the super- and subordination issue because the USUN Chief as an actor may approach his position from some moral pinnacle and ask who's boss, who rules. Even more (and I may be guilty of using literary cant), he may be an antileader, without organization or leadership of an institutionalized opposition, with no outlet for ambition nor hope of achieving higher office. He can be a national leader who has once tasted the power and the glory, with no policy program to fight for, but with followers who follow and believe. He may have status and renown as a USUN Chief and yet moan to anyone who will listen about his outcast fate. At the same time, he will be doing what he can to undermine presidentially determined foreign policy.

These are the marks of the antileader, a concept which may not suit—and rightly—systems analysis, but which just as rightly belongs in an examination of superordinate-subordinate roles in a political subsystem. It may be literary cant to talk of an antileader, but in the era of antihero, antinovel, anticulture, antidrama, antimemoir, and antinewspaper—in other words, protagonists that work for disintegration in the name of integration—no tool of analysis can be safely disregarded.

Notes

1. The source is a USUN official who cannot be identified.
2. Robert D. Murphy, *Diplomat among Warriors* (New York: Doubleday, 1964), p. 367. Murphy extricated himself from this position in less than three months.

The "Other" State Department

3. "There is probably not a single U.S. Mission . . . anywhere that is not profoundly convinced that it knows much more about what U.S. policy in its area should be than does the State Department." (Francis T. P. Plimpton, in Edward P. Doyle [ed.], *As We Knew Adlai: The Stevenson Story* [New York: Harper and Row, 1966], p. 260.)

4. Murphy, *op. cit.*, p. 368. As for Secretary Dulles' soothing comment that "if it happens again, just tell me and I'll take care of it," Murphy writes: "The American Mission's assertion of independence from the State Department continued through the eight years of the Eisenhower Administration. The political influence and exceptional ability of Ambassador Lodge gradually transformed the American delegation at the UN until, as the years passed, our mission behaved less like an embassy than a second Foreign office of the United States Government. . . . But the existence of a two-headed Foreign office is potentially dangerous because it can seriously hamper coordination of foreign policy." As an example of Lodge's pre-eminence, Dulles rid himself of four White House aides on foreign policy—C. D. Jackson, Nelson A. Rockefeller, William Jackson, and Harold Stassen—to ensure that "no competing centers of influence" between the President and himself could be established. (Ole R. Holsti, "Cognitive Dynamics and Images of the Enemy," *Journal of International Affairs*, XXI, No. 1 [1967], 36.) He could do nothing so drastic about Lodge.

5. Winthrop W. Aldrich, "The Suez Crisis: A Footnote to History," *Foreign Affairs*, XLV, No. 3 (April 1967), 541 ff. Aldrich was ambassador in London from 1953 to 1957.

6. Interview with Robert D. Murphy, former Deputy Undersecretary of State, now president, Corning Glass International, at his office, 717 Fifth Avenue, New York City. Lodge's biographer writes: "Murphy's memory of these events does not agree with Lodge's. Lodge worked under instructions day and night for almost eight years, during his whole tenure at the U.N. There was one episode which occurred at the time of the Suez crisis when Secretary Dulles was ill. A group proposed a resolution which, while very cleverly worded, seemed to Lodge in effect to be backing away from the original Eisenhower position. . . . Lodge felt that on a matter of this importance, the President himself should be informed. Lodge received a call from Bob Murphy, who was then Acting Secretary of State, supporting this resolution and asking Lodge to do so, and Lodge said he thought on a matter of this importance he ought to consult the President. He did so and the U.S. adhered to its original position." (William J. Miller, *Henry Cabot Lodge* [New York: James H. Heineman, Inc., 1967], p. 268.) This passage is reminiscent of a line in Conrad's *Victory* where the hero says: "A diplomatic state-

ment is a statement of which everything is true but the sentiment which seems to prompt it."

7. As an indication of Lodge's "strong pull with Ike," Eisenhower relates in his memoirs that after his 1952 election, he decided to appoint a White House chief of staff who "would really be Assistant President." He considered Sherman Adams and Lodge. Secretary-designate Dulles successfully urged upon the President that Lodge succeed the ailing Senator Austin as USUN Chief. (Miller, *op. cit.*, p. 257.) Sherman Adams, in *Firsthand Report* (New York: Harper and Row, 1961), p. 75, reports that the President had such confidence in Lodge that when Governor Adams discussed leaving the White House because of a better business offer elsewhere, the President considered Lodge as replacement. "After a day or two, Eisenhower called me in," writes Adams. "Lodge was happy with his work as Ambassador to the UN more than anything he had ever done." Secretary of State Lansing's difficulties with President Wilson are described in Alexander L. George and Juliette L. George, *Woodrow Wilson and Colonel House: A Personality Study* (New York: Dover, 1964), pp. 216, 249, 297.

8. Murphy is, of course, referring to Lodge's ambitions for the 1960 Presidential nomination. Lodge continued to act as a diplomatic free spirit when he became United States Ambassador in Saigon in June 1963 and presided over the liquidation of Ngo Dinh Diem's empire. According to Roger Hilsman, then Assistant Secretary of State for Far Eastern Affairs, Lodge handled the American correspondents in Saigon superbly by giving them stories he wanted to see in print. "Even in Washington," writes Hilsman, "it was clear that it was Lodge who was doing most of the leaking. The only trouble was that Lodge's interest did not always coincide with Washington's and there were times when the steady flow of all-too-revealing information leaking from Saigon drove [President] Kennedy close to distraction." (*To Move a Nation* [New York: Doubleday, 1967], p. 514.) Despite Lodge's known distaste for governmental lines of authority, his resources were of such value to a Democratic Administration that they could, apparently, outweigh putative personality deficiencies. In March 1968, President Johnson appointed Lodge ambassador to the German Federal Republic.

9. *Time*, LXXII (August 11, 1958), pp. 11–14, says that from the outset of his embassy, Lodge made it quite clear he would not be bound by orders from the International Organization Affairs office in the State Department. He frequently got his instructions changed or else wrote them himself. He argued that events at the UN happened so quickly that instructions could be outdated. Also see Robert J. Donovan, *Eisenhower: The Inside Story* (New York: Harper and Row, 1956), pp. 14 *et passim*,

for references to Lodge's intervention in domestic as well as foreign policy or UN affairs.

10. Max Beloff, *New Dimensions in Foreign Policy: A Study in Administrative Experience, 1947–1959* (New York: Macmillan, 1961), p. 176.

11. Ernest A. Gross, *Oral History Project*, Columbia University. Transcript, pp. 550 ff.

12. *Ibid.*, p. 575.

13. *Ibid.*, "Recollections of Dag Hammarskjöld as Secretary-General," p. 10.

14. Interview with Andrew Cordier, April 10, 1967, at his office, McVickar Hall, Columbia University.

15. Here we have the interaction of three leading actors and their subsystems: USUN, Secretary-General, Secretary of State.

16. Interview with Andrew Cordier.

17. Norman A. Graebner (ed.), *An Uncertain Tradition: American Secretaries of State in the Twentieth Century* (New York: McGraw-Hill, 1961), p. 256, reports that in March 1948, Ambassador Austin "seemingly reversed the President's [Truman] policy by proposing a suspension of the partition plan and agreeing that Palestine be placed under a temporary United Nations trusteeship. 'How could this have happened?' Truman asked Clark Clifford, his personal adviser, instructing him at the same time to find out how it did." Senator Austin was appointed in June 1946 as USUN Chief, but the appointment did not take effect until January 1947 at the conclusion of his Senate term. During that period, Herschel Johnson, a career State Department official, was acting Chief with Austin as his unofficial adviser. See also Walter Mills (ed.), *The Forrestal Diaries* (New York: Viking, 1951), p. 221.

18. *United States Foreign Policy: Its Organization and Control*, Report of Study Group for the Woodrow Wilson Foundation (New York: Columbia University Press, 1952), p. 54.

19. *UN Charter*, Chapter III, Article 7.

20. *White House Press Release*, July 20, 1965, also Department of State *Bulletin*, August 9, 1965, p. 240. The numerical designations are my own. According to Lodge's biographer (Miller, *op. cit.*, p. 257), President Eisenhower told Lodge: "I regard this [USUN] job as next in importance to the Secretary of State. You will rank immediately below him, and have Cabinet status. And I'll want you to sit in on meetings of the National Security Council." President Eisenhower himself has written: "The post was one of vital importance—in fact, I later accorded its occupant Cabinet rank *with a seniority just below that of the*

Secretary of State." (Dwight D. Eisenhower, *The White House Years: 1953–56* [New York: Doubleday, 1963], p. 89.) (Emphasis added.)

21. Clayton Fritchey, "Our Heroes at the U.N.," *Harper's Magazine* (February 1967), p. 34.

22. *Ibid.,* p. 30.

23. Recently, William B. Buffum, Deputy Assistant Secretary of State for International Organization Affairs, was inducted as Ambassador Goldberg's senior deputy at USUN. (*New York Times,* February 3, 1967.) This appointment has been interpreted as confirming the USUN "takeover bid" of the I.O. Bureau.

24. Richard E. Neustadt, *Presidential Power, The Politics of Leadership* (New York: John Wiley, 1960), *passim.* The MacArthur case may not be wholly analogous to the USUN-State Department "collective bargaining" scramble since MacArthur was not only pressing his personal resources as a field commander but also seeking monopoly power of command over the war's political aims. The Humphrey case may be more to the point because here we have a Cabinet officer "publicly assailing the presidential budget on the very day it was sent down" (p. 66). Stevenson, as we shall see in the next chapter, often and in direct quotation marks uttered statements which might have led to his dismissal if his resources had been less.

25. Richard N. Gardner, "The U.S. and the U.N.: An Appraisal of Our National Interest," *Harvard Today* (Spring 1963), pp. 2–8. Cited in Martin C. Needler (ed.), *Dimensions of American Foreign Policy: Readings and Documents* (Princeton: Van Nostrand, 1966).

26. J. Leiper Freeman, *The Political Process: Executive Bureau-Legislative Committee Relations* (rev. ed.; New York: Random House, 1965), p. 10: "Subsystem . . . refers to the pattern of interactions of participants, or actors, involved in making decisions in a special area of public policy. Furthermore, although there are obviously other types of subsystems, the type which concerns us here is found in an immediate setting formed by an executive bureau and congressional committees, with special interest groups intimately attached."

8/ The USUN Chief

One Friday afternoon early in December 1966, Assistant Secretary of State Joseph Sisco was presented to a crowded State Department auditorium as the substitute speaker for Ambassador Goldberg, who could not be in Washington. Scheduled to address a semiannual briefing session for news media representatives from all over the country December 2, Goldberg had canceled the date so as to remain in New York to attend upon the re-election of U Thant as Secretary-General.

The auditorium was jammed with radio, TV, and newspaper writers who normally leave the two-day briefing session after lunch to return home. They had stayed on, quite obviously, to hear Goldberg and to question him, as they had other speakers at these semiannual briefing sessions. With the announcement that Sisco would act as Goldberg's surrogate, there began an exodus. By the time Sisco had finished his address, his audience had been sharply reduced. An outstanding Foreign Service officer with years of experience and an academic background, Sisco is an excellent and forceful speaker. It did not matter. The Ambassador was the man they wanted to hear, and no one else would do.[1]

Lack of resources is the Assistant Secretary's handicap in carrying out his assigned duties. When the USUN Chief is a two-time candidate for President or a former United States Supreme Court Justice; or when he sits as a Cabinet colleague with the Assistant Secretary's superior, the Secretary of State; or when the USUN Chief of Mission, the Deputy Ambassador, and the Counselor have three hot lines (to the Texas White House, the Washington White House, and the Pentagon); when the Ambassador is a Presidential guest at Camp David (during which he helps to settle an important labor dispute during its prestrike phase) or when he is a former Undersecretary of State who is recalled to public service by the President —it becomes difficult for an Assistant Secretary to over-awe the Ambassador with any modernized version of "le Roi le veult" unless "le Roi" happens to be the President himself.

These observations are not startlingly new to some observers. For example, at Ambassador Goldberg's first press conference after taking office, there occurred the following colloquy:

Q.—Do you consider that you are acting under instructions from the State Department or as coequal to the Secretary of State?

A.—I haven't the slightest bit of interest in jurisdictional matters. . . . I was appointed by the President. I have the most cordial relations with my old Cabinet colleague Dean Rusk. I do not anticipate there will be the slightest bit of difficulty in this area. And I am not going to draw an organization chart to plot the path that here I have to follow.[2]

The case of Adlai Stevenson illustrates a different kind of ambassadorial resource to be illustrated later by an attempt at case history. Stevenson's resource was negative because, while he lacked President Kennedy's wholehearted trust and favor, his national following was measurably significant—not enough to elect him President, but substantial enough for President Kennedy to want him to stay on at the UN.[3]

Stevenson's tenure raises important questions about the post. Why do prominent Americans take this assignment, and why are they selected for it by the Chief Executive? Senator Austin had been a member of the Foreign Relations Committee and one of the leading Republican influences, along with Senator Vandenberg, in inculcating a sense of internationalism into the G.O.P. No other Republican Senator was ready to leave the Senate for this post, but "Austin was very interested in the job."[4] He was willing to serve under a Democratic President. The Republican leadership regarded his appointment as a natural concomitant of bipartisanship in foreign policy, even though they were raking President Truman over the coals for being "soft" on Communism. Nevertheless Austin's almost religious conviction about the Charter gave great weight to his influence with Congress about UN affairs. We have already seen how much Senator Lodge relished his UN post. Stevenson badly wanted to be Secretary of State, but could not get the designation.[5] He took the next best thing for a man deeply interested in foreign affairs who had a long and early involvement with the United Nations.[6]

As for Justice Goldberg, his willingness to take the job may be the outgrowth of an energetic personality which found little outlet in the Supreme Court. But it was his decision.[7] Of the four men cited, only one, Ambassador Lodge, saw in this post a path to higher elective political office. For Senator Austin, Ambassador Stevenson (*faute de mieux?*), and Justice Goldberg, it would appear that the USUN chieftaincy was reward in itself and a fitting climax to a public career. From a personality standpoint, the position was satisfying to anyone who wanted visibility. In the winter of 1965, President Johnson sent Goldberg on a tour of European capitals and the Vatican on a "peace offensive" against North Vietnam. Secretary Rusk would have been wasted on such a trip, if only because he did not carry with him the "UN image." Thus whatever temporary political benefits were reaped by President Johnson came about because his emissary had attached to his title the emotive phrase, "United Nations."[8]

There are few diplomatic posts in the American government that permit an officeholder such an awesome amount of world publicity as came to Goldberg during his unproductive trip through western Europe and during the 1967 Middle East crisis. Sumner Welles made an exploratory trip for President Roosevelt in the early months of World War II, but purely as a State Department official. Goldberg, however, carried the UN shield.

Why Ambassador Ball accepted the post is something of a mystery. During his five years as Undersecretary of State in the Kennedy and Johnson administrations, he was regarded as less than an admirer of the UN. A man of high intellectual distinction, Ball left the State Department in October 1966 after three decades of generalized involvement in American foreign policy as private citizen and public official. During the fifties he was a law partner of Adlai Stevenson, counsel to Jean Monnet and the European Economic Communities in that halcyon pre-De Gaulle era of European unification. When President Johnson persuaded him in April 1968 to take the USUN Post, Ball was chairman of Lehman Bros. International Ltd.

What makes Ball's appointment so intriguing is that he was at odds with major aspects of American foreign policy during his service as a high policy-making official. His book *The Discipline of Power*, published in Spring 1968, documents his disagreements with Johnson and Secretary Rusk on Vietnam, Communist China, SEATO obligations of the United States, the UN and the United States "special relationship" with Britain. He has been particularly critical of USUN policy-making prerogatives. He has disagreed strongly with United States policy toward South Africa and United States over-concern about Africa. He is a strongly "Europe-oriented" American diplomat who aroused strong criticism among Asian and African delegates at the organizing session in Geneva June 1964 of the UN Conference on Trade and Development for his blunt, tough words on United States foreign economic policy vis-à-vis the less developed third world.

Despite what would seem to be "ideological" disqualifications for the USUN post, Johnson pressed it on him and Ball accepted it even though—or, perhaps, because— the term in June 1968, when he was officially to enter upon his duties, had barely eight months to run. While Ball surely lacked the large public constituency of Stevenson or the narrow but still large constituency of Goldberg, he had the confidence of those publics concerned with foreign policy. And once more we saw a President selecting as his spokesman at the UN a non-career professional with independent ideas and a will to express them with irreproachable candor.

In discussing USUN executives, it is important to distinguish their formal, institutionalized roles ("positional-ascriptive") from their performance, their style of operation ("behaviorally descriptive").[9] In this fashion and with as many behavior examples as possible, patterns common to the position they held can be uncovered.

As noted earlier, the USUN is out in the open, like the UN. It is a sight-seeing tourist attraction of political as well as, perhaps, esthetic interest. The Mission itself is involved with various publics, dealing not merely with press and other media but with groups of people who come regularly to the USUN for briefing sessions. During 1966 the USUN conducted 375 briefings in its small auditorium before a total of eighteen thousand people, or more than one briefing a day.[10] And, of course, there are the thousands of visitors, particularly school children in chartered busses, coming to the UN each day for the tour of the building.

A close friend of President Johnson, one who could be described as a "participant-observer" in the UN-USUN subsystem, once told him that the USUN Chief should meet three requirements:

1. He should be eminent, not a lame duck.

2. He should have the President's personal ear.

3. He should not be a career diplomat because he is not trained in multilateral diplomacy.

It would be difficult to call Stevenson or Lodge lame ducks, even though the latter had been defeated for re-election to the Senate in 1952. Even if Stevenson did not have President Kennedy's ear all the time, the President still had to listen to him occasionally if only to avoid public difficulties with him. As for point three, a Senator, a labor-management negotiator, or an elected official with a UN background can claim to understand multilateralism, if not in its diplomatic aspect, at least in its "legislative" aspect. And though Ball made no pretense of being a "multilateralist"—his book indicates his acceptance of a bipolar world for the foreseeable future—his enormous intelligence, personal charm, and international legal training were certain to enlist his uncomplicated adherence to this still unique method of diplomatic negotiation.

The USUN Chief's role, in my opinion, has not been clearly visualized by those who have studied modern American diplomacy. For example, the staff report to the Jackson subcommittee declared, "Of the Cabinet members, only a Secretary of State is primarily charged with looking at the Nation as a whole in relation to the world."[11] Yet the USUN Chief not only has that task but is also charged with looking at the nations of the world in relation to the nation. As the "UN Ambassador" to the United States, he mediates between the State Department and the UN, between the nation and the "nations." Among the President's many roles, says Clinton Rossiter, is that of Chief Diplomat.[12] Can one then describe the Secretary of State as the "Associate Chief Diplomat" and the USUN representative as "Assistant Chief Diplomat"? The fact that this is not an absurd rhetorical question (even though it may not be answered precisely) indicates that the USUN Chief transcends the positional-ascriptive role within the policy process.[13]

With the exception of at most four Cabinet Secretaries —State, Defense, Treasury, and the Attorney-General—

the USUN Chief with his Cabinet status is far better known than other departmental heads, for whose activities there is no generalized sustained interest. The Secretary of Agriculture (or Commerce or Labor), for example, runs a specialized department of administration primarily for special-interest groups. So do other Cabinet members except HEW, perhaps. Their appointment by the President is rarely due to their national eminence; more frequently it is the outgrowth of agreements made before Presidential nominations.

Richard F. Fenno, Jr., has written about the relationship of President to Cabinet officer:

> *If a Cabinet member has a national standing among a particular public which is sufficient to make the President more effective than he otherwise would be, he has an increment of prestige which is independent of that which the President has. . . . To the extent that the Cabinet member does not owe his prestige to the President, he may have a sphere of activity relatively free from presidential control.*[14]

Neither Senator Austin, Goldberg, nor Stevenson owed his individual prestige to the three Presidents involved.[15] They were nationally known personalities well before their designations and of specific personal value to their Chief Executive. How significant their Cabinet rank may be is difficult to measure.[16] Whether or not Cabinet rank for the USUN Chief is a good thing was asked by Clayton Fritchey:

> *This extra status has, if anything, made matters worse for it encourages the press to treat them as independent policy*

*makers, which inevitably leads to unfortunate publicity when
the views (real or imagined) of the Ambassador are disregarded by the Administration.*[17]

Actually Cabinet status means little to a USUN Chief
because as a collectivity, the institution today means less
and less. It has been noted that Goldberg missed about
one-half the Cabinet sessions because, as one USUN
official put it, "he felt that he could accomplish more right
up here at the UN than down in Washington."

If one may introduce a conspiratorial note here, from
the standpoint of the Secretary of State or the President
it may not be such a bad idea to allow the USUN Chief
to be (or to seem) freewheeling, to gain a reputation for
independence. A favorite hobby of demonological liberals
or conservatives is to attack the Secretary of State for
derelictions more properly attributable to the Chief Executive.[18] How nice it is for both men when the USUN
Chief or some other subordinate is attacked by interested
publics *pour encourager les autres.* In several cases, Lodge
was blamed for the United States hands-off attitude during the Hungarian crisis, most notably by *Life* magazine.
Stevenson was blamed for allegedly persuading President
Kennedy to call off the air cover during the Spring 1961
invasion of Cuba. Goldberg is blamed by pro-South
African lobbyists for the verbal alteration in United
States policy toward Pretoria.

In a moment of mock despair, James Q. Wilson has
written that since most foreign policy problems are insoluble, "any Secretary of State will cease trying to solve

[them]."[19] In such a case, what better than to have the drama of the UN and the USUN enacted right before the public gaze, knowing all the while that nothing serious will happen? Alas, those who propound such Machiavellian notions do not realize that politicians, statesmen, nations, and even supernations can become prisoners of their own rhetoric after two decades of repetition on all critical as well as ceremonial occasions.

I have seen the Deputy Ambassador of a major Western country patiently and amiably seeking to explain to the young Ambassador from an East African country the reasons for voting against a resolution favored by that analytic concept called "Africa." The East African diplomat was strident in his disagreement and made it clear he was not buying propaganda. What makes this particularly wondrous is that the African, despite his imposing rank at the UN, is a very low man on the country's totem pole. Nevertheless, the UN is a place where all nations are equal and therefore all the delegations are equal and therefore all votes are equal.[20]

Critics of the USUN Chief and the Mission itself say that if they stay on too long, they become "UNationized" (pronounced "you-enationized"), a pejorative neologism intended to demonstrate that a limit should be placed on the length of service of a UN delegate. As another participant-observer put it:

Here it's all words, words, words. If you knew the amount of work which went into the fighting over whether the resolution words should be "recalling," "mindful of," "reaffirming," "requests," "urges," "calls upon," "demands," "regrets," "deplores," "condemns," "denounces"—it's unbelievable. The number of word changes in the resolution on Southwest Africa[21] was in the hundreds and hundreds. Eventually you begin to believe these words are important.

With all this description of action and interaction, of subsystems penetrating and interpenetrating one another, an important question remains: the reason for all this activity. Amitai Etzioni has written, "Organizations are social units predominantly oriented to attainment of specific goals."[22]

What are the specific goals of a USUN Chief? Are they separable from the USUN itself? Can these specific goals be harmonized with the specific goals of another social unit, the Department of State?

We can examine the Chief of Mission roles more easily than the roles of others in his subsystem because he is far more in the open, more accessible, more in an arena than other diplomats of greater or equal stature. It is to the story of Adlai Stevenson that I want now to turn to see if we can establish the meaning of the USUN during his incumbency from 1961 to his death in July 1965.

Notes

1. The incident described is autoptic.
2. Department of State *Bulletin,* August 16, 1965, p. 277. The date of the press conference was July 28, 1965. Quite obviously, Ambassador

Goldberg, who as a Supreme Court Justice managed to find his way to the heart of a question, was unable or unwilling to answer a direct question about instructions, quite reminiscent of the Lodge-Murphy colloquy referred to earlier. It is inconceivable that any other United States ambassador could be asked such a question or, in the unlikely event that he were asked, that he would risk such an insubordinate answer. Yet why should Goldberg have answered any differently, when six months later he could talk about exacting "only one commitment from the President of the United States when he asked me to take this post" (see Chapter 10). In the words of Marshal Juin, "La discipline des Maréchaux n'est pas celle des sergents."

3. Stevenson received 27.3 million votes (to General Eisenhower's 33.9 million) in 1952 and 26 million to 35.6 in 1956. As for President Kennedy's desire to have Stevenson at the UN, see the biography by Theodore Sorenson, *Kennedy* (New York: Bantam, 1966), p. 284: "Even personality problems cropped up. [Kennedy] was, for example, irritated by Stevenson's delay in deciding on the UN Ambassadorship and publicly announced that it had been offered in order to make rejection all the more difficult."

4. Ernest A. Gross, *Oral History Project*, Columbia University. Transcript, p. 535. It was Dean Acheson, then Undersecretary of State, who sensing a Republican victory in Congress in 1946 urged upon Secretary of State Byrnes nomination of a Republican "internationalist" senator like Austin to head USUN. Byrnes agreed and made the recommendation to President Truman. This was an attempt to ensure the bipartisan tradition in foreign policy and to enhance the USUN post by giving it to a prominent public figure like Austin. I am indebted to Dr. Joseph Johnson for this information.

5. Arthur M. Schlesinger, Jr., confirmed to me in an interview March 4, 1967, the statement made by a friend of Stevenson's: "Adlai had refused to nominate JFK in 1960 and that may have cost him the Secretary of State appointment." Another version has it that after Kennedy's primary victory over Hubert Humphrey in West Virginia, Kennedy asked Stevenson for his support, but "Stevenson demurred, saying he wanted to remain 'neutral' so he could act as a middleman between Kennedy and [Senate Majority Leader] Johnson when the new administration took office. That embittered Kennedy. 'I am being turned down right and left,' he told a friend, adding, 'I don't mind. But how could I make Stevenson Secretary of State after this absurd performance? How could he serve as a go-between when Johnson has no use for him and regards him as a weakling?" (Edward Weintal and Charles Bartlett, *Facing The Brink* [New York: Scribner, 1967], p. 145.)

6. Stevenson was assistant to Secretary of State Stettinius and adviser to the United States delegation at San Francisco in 1945; chief of the United States delegation to the UN Preparatory Commission, London, 1946; and a member of the United States delegation at the first and second General Assemblies in 1946 and 1947. (Edward P. Doyle [ed.], *As We Knew Adlai: The Stevenson Story* [New York: Harper and Row, 1966], p. 254.) Stevenson was called out to San Francisco by Stettinius in May 1945 when the United States press began to criticize the United States delegation for not having a press spokesman. Stevenson attended the delegation meetings and "used his own judgment about what to say to the twenty-odd reporters who were admitted to his 'leak office.' As a result relations with the press improved and there was better reporting of the American position." Stevenson was Stettinius' deputy at the London preparatory conference, and when the latter became ill, Stevenson became delegation chairman. (Norman A. Graebner [ed.], *An Uncertain Tradition: American Secretaries of State in the Twentieth Century* [New York: McGraw-Hill, 1961], pp. 220, 221.)

7. Transcript of remarks by Ambassador Goldberg at luncheon of UN Correspondents Association, United Nations, April 20, 1967 (*USUN Press Release 46*): "Nobody twisted my arm to come down here. As persuasive as President Johnson is, he cannot twist the arm of a Justice of the Supreme Court. That is beyond his power. So I came down here of my own volition."

8. It may have some significance that Ambassador Goldberg's statement in fall 1966 on Vietnam at the UN was circularized by the State Department as the official United States policy declaration and that United States Ambassadors "were instructed to communicate that fact to all governments, including our adversaries in Vietnam." (Transcript of remarks by Ambassador Goldberg, *ibid.*, p. 14.) Similarly, President Johnson's speech June 19, 1967, and subsequent speeches by Goldberg were circulated to all United States embassies as official policy statements on the Middle East.

9. Lewis J. Edinger, *Kurt Schumacher: A Study in Personality and Political Behavior* (Stanford, Calif.: Stanford University Press, 1965), p. 4. Edinger is, of course, discussing leadership, but what he writes is pertinent to the USUN "leader": "Neither individual character structure nor the contextual configuration can by itself explain a leader's behavior; but careful analysis of their interaction, in as many instances as possible, may reveal certain patterns and facilitate understanding."

10. USUN-published sources (mimeo). Some twenty members of the Mission are called upon regularly to brief delegations which come by

appointment. In a period of several weeks, USUN briefing officers met with groups from the Methodist Youth Fellowship, Foreign Policy Association, American Jewish Congress, League of Women Voters, and a number of student delegations from metropolitan colleges. There is a question-and-answer period after the lecture.

11. Henry M. Jackson (ed.), *The Secretary of State and the Ambassador* (New York: Praeger, 1964), p. 13.

12. Clinton Rossiter, *The American Presidency* (2d ed., rev.; New York: New American Library, 1960), p. 23.

13. Goldberg was once asked whether he would not prefer a title of higher-sounding rank, such as Undersecretary of State for UN Affairs. He firmly replied that he was satisfied to be called Ambassador because his status arose not as concomitant to a title but from his relationship with the President—the sovereign. Becoming part of the State Department chain of command, no matter how high up in the hierarchical structure, would not be "helpful." Philip M. Klutznick, a non-career professional who served as a USUN ambassador under Stevenson, has argued, however, that the USUN Chief should be made an Undersecretary of State, administratively responsible to the Secretary of State with the Assistant Secretary for I.O. responsible to the Ambassador. He said: "The State Department might then begin to feel that the U.S. Mission is not an enemy in its midst. It should create a feeling of camaraderie between New York and Washington which is so essential to our foreign policy performance." The changes proposed by Klutznick would necessitate amendments to the Participation Act. It is doubtful that anybody in any branch of government would relish opening up the act to amendments. (Philip M. Klutznick, "The UN, A Casualty of Vietnam and the Middle East," speech before annual meeting of the United Nations Association, January 18, 1968, Chicago, Ill., p. 8.)

14. Richard F. Fenno, Jr., *The President's Cabinet.* (Cambridge, Mass.: Harvard University Press, 1959), p. 178. Fenno points out that President Roosevelt retained Jesse Jones in the Cabinet "because his presence was helpful—not in spite of his independent strength, but because of it."

15. I have omitted Lodge because what "prestige" he had in 1953 was due to his personal relationship with President Eisenhower, not to any spectacular long-term political achievement.

16. Under President Kennedy, Cabinet meetings were few. Under President Johnson, these conclaves in no way exemplify one of the Administration's favorite political word-symbols—"dialogue," or the more exhortatory, "Let us reason together." How little President John-

son thinks of his Cabinet came out in a private conversation discussing the political value of some of his Cabinet officers. Reportedly, he said that "they couldn't find their way to a polling-booth without seeing-eye dogs." Being a Republican, Senator Austin did not sit in the Truman Cabinet.

17. Clayton Fritchey, "Our Heroes at the U.N.," *Harper's Magazine* (February 1967), p. 32. It is not only the press which is so encouraged but also special-interest groups. For instance, in spring 1966, Goldberg received a large group of American Negro leaders who discussed with him United States policy on South Africa and Rhodesia. Later one of the visitors criticized Goldberg for what was regarded as lukewarm support of the African position toward these two all-white regimes. When another remonstrated that Goldberg had no alternative as Ambassador but to support the United States rather than the African position, the first visitor said: "He shouldn't have taken the job of Ambassador if he has to agree with them in Washington."

"Our trial interviews revealed that in addition to this source of conflicting expectations, actors frequently were exposed to incongruent expectations as incumbents of single positions." Neal Gross, Ward S. Mason, Alexander M. McEachern, *Explorations in Role Analysis: Studies of the School Superintendency Role* (New York: John Wiley & Sons, 1964), p. 5.

18. Secretary Hull was a target for F.D.R.'s refusal to support Republican Spain against Franco. Secretary Marshall was blamed for dilatory tactics in recognizing Israel. Secretary Acheson was blamed for many things. Assistant Secretary Adolf A. Berle in his day was attacked for supporting "Fascists" in Latin America, while Robert Murphy was denounced in 1942 for the so-called deal with Admiral Darlan in North Africa.

19. James Q. Wilson, "The Bureaucracy Problem," *The Public Interest*, No. 6 (Winter 1967), p. 6: "It is regrettable, for example, that any country must have a foreign office since none can have a good one. The reason is simple: it is literally impossible to have a 'policy' with respect to *all* [original emphasis] foreign countries, much less a consistent and reasonable policy. And the difficulty increases with the square of the number of countries, and probably with the cube of the speed of communications. The problem long ago became insoluble and any sensible Secretary of State ceases trying to solve it. He will divide his time instead between ad hoc responses to the crisis of the moment and appearances on Meet the Press." Rusk was once asked if his ambition was to go down in history as the Secretary who had solved the Berlin crisis. Very sensibly by Wilson's standard, Rusk replied:

"No, I'm not that vain. But I want to go down in history as one of those Secretaries of State who succeeded in passing the Berlin crisis on to his successor." (Roger Hilsman, *To Move a Nation* [New York: Doubleday, 1967], p. 41.)

20. A "participant-observer" at USUN has told me: "What makes the job of the Mission Chief so arduous and time-consuming is that when any one of the 123 other ambassadors want to see him, you can't settle for anybody of lesser rank. It's ambassador-to-ambassador relationships which count and you never can tell when you're going to need somebody's vote and if you've palmed off an ambassador on a political officer when he wanted Goldberg, you may whistle for his vote when you need it."

21. Francis T. M. Plimpton writes (Doyle, *op. cit.*, p. 256) that the UN acts "by resolution and resolutions are words, words fought over, dissected, shaded, sharpened, blunted, fused or defused." The resolution referred to above is No. 2145 of the 21st General Assembly, October 27, 1966, which nullified South Africa's mandate over Southwest Africa.

22. Amitai Etzioni, *Complex Organizations: A Sociological Reader* (New York: Holt, Rinehart and Winston, 1965), p. vii.

9/ Adlai Stevenson: 1961–1965

Mrs. Edison Dick, a long-time friend of Adlai Stevenson, talked to him during the Bay of Pigs crisis, and she quotes him as follows:

When I asked him what was wrong, he said quietly: "You heard my speech [at the UN] today? Well, I did not tell the whole truth; I did not know the whole truth. I took this job at the President's request on the understanding that I would be consulted and kept fully informed on everything. I spoke in the United Nations in good faith on that understanding. Now my credibility has been compromised, and therefore my usefulness. Yet how can I resign at this moment and make things still worse for the President?[1]

This was the story of the Bay of Pigs invasion in April 1961 when Ambassador Stevenson was denying at the UN any United States complicity in an invasion of Cuba by exiles. Days later, he learned that he had not been told the whole truth. The plain fact of the matter is that Stevenson was lied to, or so he and his associates at USUN believed.[2] President Kennedy explained it all later to Stevenson as "a communications failure."

The Bay of Pigs contretemps was only one of several instances in which the White House-State Department-USUN-UN interacted in ways to make the Weberian concept of unintended consequences seem like understatement. From the standpoint of sound administration, it was probably a good thing to assign Stevenson's friend, admirer, and confidant, Arthur M. Schlesinger, Jr., "the official role . . . of White House liaison" with Stevenson.[3] Schlesinger could act as a sympathetic audience for the USUN Chief, who, "enveloped in the United Nations-New York atmosphere where world opinion weighed heavier than domestic, felt out of touch with decisions in Washington."[4] To Schlesinger's office at the White House came many letters from Stevenson on many issues of foreign policy. How much influence his letters had on the White House is hard to say, though even among Stevenson's friends there is doubt that President Kennedy paid much attention to them. Occasionally, he might take Stevenson's opinion where it did not affect any substantive matter.[5]

Another and, perhaps, more important liaison officer with Stevenson was Assistant Secretary Harlan M. Cleve-

land, in charge of the I.O. Bureau. The relationship between these men was close and warm, all the more so
because Cleveland was a political writer of note and a
man of intellectual attainment. The USUN Chief, according to his friends, was always in touch with Cleveland.
There is some dispute among several sources as to how
deeply Stevenson involved himself in UN issues. The
consensus seems to be that he involved himself to a lesser
degree than Lodge or Goldberg. As one observer put it,
"Adlai was no big fighter with State on policy." Speeches
were often drafted in Washington, sent to New York for
re-editing, and then returned to Washington for approval.
With Ambassador Goldberg, speech drafts were initiated
in New York. "We're getting in the first word and they're
[Washington] redrafting, instead of as before when
Washington sent off the first draft," said a USUN official
who spanned both the Stevenson and Goldberg embassies.[6]
He continued:

*It is better if you have a draft; then the bureaucracy has
to work on your version. For example, if Goldberg has
troubles with State on his ideas for a speech and if they tell
him that the last four-fifths of his speech are being made at
the wrong time, he bounces back and says: Okay, we'll try it
another way. If he gets a no again, he says: Okay, let's try it
another way. He wears down the bureaucracy, unlike Adlai
who didn't care what was said so long as it was said properly.
For Stevenson language was important, and when he had to
work on a speech, he shut the door of his office and he could*

*not be interrupted until he had finished. To Goldberg, ideas
are tools to achieve ends. He's not a word man.*

Stevenson, however, had something which no ambassador before him or since has had: national leadership and a loyal constituency. Whether the President liked him or not, he had to be given some consideration, at least in how he was handled.[7] After the Bay of Pigs "communications break" the Kennedy-Stevenson relationship is seen in a different light by Schlesinger:

And, though Kennedy expected a certain softness in Stevenson's recommendations and was occasionally ironic about this, too, he knew that his ambassador to the UN had to be responsive to his constituency and on balance welcomed Stevenson's advocacy of the claims of American idealism and of the international community if only to counterbalance the hard-nosed Europe-obsessed mood of the State Department.[8]

Stevenson knew how he stood with President Kennedy, but he knew it even more when he was attacked by a "leak" in an article published in the *Saturday Evening Post* in the aftermath of the Cuban missile crisis in October 1962.[9] Still he stayed on. A Stevenson friend reports:

Adlai was furious at the story because it was an obvious plant. Thousands of letters and telegrams came in supporting Adlai. There were editorials supporting him even in papers which had been anti-Adlai. Clayton Fritchey [then public affairs officer at the Mission] was responsible for all the support, although a good deal of it was spontaneous. Fritchey telephoned editors all over the country telling them the issue was not whether or not they liked Adlai but whether meetings of the National Security Council were to be inviolate or not, or whether the President was not in danger of being surrounded by yes-men, if there were leaks out of the National Security Council.[10]

In actual fact, Stevenson was sharply criticized within the Administration during the perilous days of October 1962 when the missile crisis was building up to the great climax. He had urged the President to "consider offering to withdraw from Guantánamo naval base as part of a plan to demilitarize, neutralize and guarantee the territorial integrity of Cuba," writes Elie Abel.[11] "Stevenson held that Guantánamo, in any event, was of little value. He also forecast grave difficulties concerning the Jupiter base in Turkey." Stevenson's recommendations were "sharply attacked" by Treasury Secretary Douglas Dillon, CIA Director John A. McCone, and former Defense Secretary Robert Lovett.[12] Paul Nitze, then Assistant Secretary of Defense for International Security Affairs, is quoted by Abel as saying that "Adlai had to be the one who looked at this proposition from the U.N. standpoint, the standpoint of simple equities and the hazards of war." As a result of all this, "Robert Kennedy decided Stevenson lacked the toughness to deal effectively with the Russians at the U.N. in liquidating the missile crisis." Robert Kennedy suggested that John J. McCloy or Herman Phleger, onetime Dulles' chief legal adviser, be sent to backstop Stevenson at the UN Security Council session.[13]

Thus there appeared on television screens Thursday afternoon, October 25, 1962, in the Security Council chamber, seated, arms folded, behind Ambassador Stevenson, John J. McCloy. After the crisis was settled, Stevenson's friends regarded the McCloy appointment as a reflection upon the Ambassador, who did little more publicly to show his displeasure with the Administration than allowing himself to be quoted by an American journalist in a British magazine of small circulation.[14]

The Kennedy-Stevenson relationship clearly confirmed that the USUN Chief had become a figure who transcended the normal boundaries of policy-making. When a President of the United States and his brother, the Attorney-General, and powerful men in and out of the Administration find it necessary to gang up, no matter what the reason, against an Ambassador who, it will be recalled, "shall hold office at the pleasure of the President," it is obvious that whatever had been intended in the creation of the USUN and its Chief, both the post and its occupant, had far exceeded the expectations of Congress and the White House. The development might well be considered dysfunctional to the intention, and yet it might be argued that what had happened was that the function of the USUN as an institution had changed in a way corresponding to the changes in the UN itself, and to the even greater changes in America's international responsibilities.

The Article 19 Controversy

What might have happened to the Kennedy-Stevenson relationship had both men survived is pure conjecture. Ambassador Stevenson did serve under another President from November 1963 to July 1965, and it was during that period that he overturned Administration policy toward the UN and the USSR.[15]

Article 19 of the UN Charter declares:

A member of the United Nations which is in arrears in the payment of its financial contributions to the Organization shall have no vote in the General Assembly if the amount of its arrears equals or exceeds the amount of the contributions due from it for the preceding two full years. The General Assembly, may, nevertheless, permit such a Member to vote if it is satisfied that the failure to pay is due to conditions beyond the control of the Member.

On June 30, 1964, the peace-keeping phase of the United Nations Congo operations ended with a huge deficit. The Soviet Union on that date owed as follows:

UN emergency budget	$ 2,145,051
UN Emergency Force	15,638,166
Congo operation	36,984,971
Total	$54,768,188[16]

There is no need to go into great detail about the origin of both peace-keeping operations except to say that they were launched with the approval or acquiescence of the

Soviet Union and France. The General Assembly vote establishing UNEF was 57 to 0 with 19 abstentions. The Congo force was established by the Security Council with the Soviet Union voting for it and subsequently by a large General Assembly majority, which also voted at the outset to finance the operations by assessments on UN members. By the end of 1961, arrears in payments were more than $100 million. Something had to be done.

A three-part plan was negotiated between the Secretary-General and the USUN with Administration support and was adopted by the General Assembly, 58 to 13 with 24 abstentions.[17] The United States was at this time paying about half of the $120 million-a-year operation and a bit less toward the $20 million Suez UNEF operation. Congress was expressing its dissent from such a one-sided fiscal policy. The dissent sharpened when the UN bond issue came up in which the United States was being asked to subscribe to one-half the bonds. To get the bond issue settled, enforcement of Article 19 became a commitment to Congress because Congress would not have approved the bond purchases without an agreement that the defaulting countries would either meet their financial obligations or lose their vote under Article 19. The commitment to enforce Article 19 was entered into with the support of every American official in Washington and New York who had responsibility in the matter: President Kennedy, Secretary Rusk, Ambassadors Stevenson, Plimpton, and Philip M. Klutznick, and Assistant Secretary of State Harlan Cleveland.[18] And supporting this high-level decision was the decision July 20, 1962, by the International Court of Justice that under Articles 11, 14, and 17 of the Charter, the General Assembly was empowered to finance peace-keeping operations. The Assembly by a vote of 76 to 17 (8 abstentions) accepted the Court's opinion December 19, 1962.[19]

Early in 1964, the United States undertook to negotiate a solution with the Soviet Union on the Article 19 impasse, in an attempt to avoid injury to the East-West "bridge-building" policies then beginning to take shape. On March 6, 1964, Ambassador Stevenson proposed to Soviet Ambassador Fedorenko a compromise under which the Soviets would pay an amount sufficient to satisfy the Article 19 requirement while at the same time receiving assurances that in the future they would not be asked to pay for operations which they did not approve of. This was the beginning of the idea of a voluntary "rescue fund" to restore the UN's solvency. On March 21, the Soviets rejected the proposed settlement. On July 10, 1964, the Soviet Union issued a document to UN members confirming this position.[20] Congress now got into the act again by passing a joint resolution calling upon USUN Chief Stevenson to ensure that defaulting countries paid up or Article 19 was applied. This resolution was sponsored by two House members who had been on the United States delegation to the 1963 Assembly, Mrs. Edna Kelly and Representative William Mailliard.

With the 19th Session convocation approaching, word began to circulate that the United States government and Stevenson were having second thoughts about enforcement of Article 19. The credibility of the Article 19 sanction was rapidly declining.[21]

A number of high-level meetings took place in Washington and New York, attended by Secretary Rusk and Ambassador Stevenson with their respective senior aides. President Johnson was apprised of the problem and alternatives:

1. Disengagement from Article 19.
2. Enforcement of Article 19.

Alternative number one meant "domestic political consequences" entailing (*a*) an uproar in Congress and (*b*) exploitation of the United States backdown by the Republican opposition. The second alternative could lead to a deterioration of United States-Soviet relations. A procedural approach was worked out to stick with the second alternative, but with much preliminary maneuvering so as to avoid, unless absolutely necessary, the actual enforcement of Article 19. It is important to note here that neither Stevenson nor anyone else proposed recommending disengagement to President Johnson.

To make credible the Article 19 sanction, the USUN circulated a memorandum to UN members October 8, 1964, outlining the United States position on Article 19 and emphasizing the serious consequences which would follow if the Article were breached. Even more significantly, a telegram was dispatched early in November 1964 to virtually every American Embassy, other than those in France and the Communist countries, instructing our ambassadors to warn their host countries that failure to support Article 19 would have the most serious adverse consequences not only on United States support for the UN but also on United States relations with their countries. The telegram represented weeks of negotiation between USUN and the State Department and was finally cleared personally by Secretary Rusk after agreement with the USUN. This telegram was followed November 16, 1964, by a United States announcement that it would not make its usual pledge of a voluntary contribution for 1965 at the annual pledging conference of the UN Special Fund and Expanded Program of Technical Assistance.[22] The announcement was made by Ambassador Franklin H. Williams, then United States representative to the Economic and Social Council, after joint approval by the USUN and State Department. While the attempt was being made to establish the credibility of the sanction, USUN spokesmen were undercutting the policy by privately suggesting to UN delegations that a compromise could be worked out. To this end the United States took the initiative to postpone the Assembly opening date from November 10 to December 1, 1964.

We now come to the climax.

Friday, November 20, 1964, Jacob Malik, a ranking Soviet Foreign Ministry official and presently Soviet representative at the UN, while visiting Ghana hinted to Ghanaian officials there that the USSR might be ready to consider the voluntary "rescue fund" proposal. He reportedly urged Accra to support the "rescue fund" compromise. This information was reported to the United States Embassy in Accra and relayed to USUN.

Friday, November 20, 1964—the same day—Stevenson *on his own initiative* arranged a meeting with Ambassador Fedorenko in New York to discuss ways and means of avoiding an Article 19 confrontation. Fedorenko noted with pleasure that Stevenson was now "singing a better tune." Fedorenko in New York rejected the "rescue fund" compromise, while Malik was talking it up in Accra. Suppose, Fedorenko said, the UN membership asked for a postponement of consideration of Article 19. What then? Stevenson replied that the issue could be postponed until the following March 1965 by dispensing with voting altogether. Perhaps the Assembly session itself could be postponed. One of Fedorenko's aides, Fedoseev, suggested a "symbolic" Assembly while negotiations went ahead. Stevenson's deputy, Ambassador Plimpton, asked how one could have an Assembly session without voting. Anything was possible under heaven, said Fedoseev. The meeting ended inconclusively, but as one informant-observer told me, "We were eyeball-to-eyeball and this time it was *our* gladiator who blinked."

Stevenson reported approvingly that the Russians were interested in the idea of a General Assembly without voting. It should be made clear that Stevenson had arranged his meeting with Fedorenko and had made his proposals to him with no forewarning or foreknowledge to the State Department and the I.O. Bureau. His telegraphed report to the State Department Friday evening on his Fedorenko interview in the afternoon came as a total surprise and shock to Washington officials. In effect, a position to which the United States had committed itself unreservedly in innumerable public statements over two years was suddenly changed despite months of meetings between USUN and the Department.

The next morning, Saturday, November 21, 1964, Stevenson breakfasted with Rusk and urged upon Rusk adoption of the no-voting proposal. Rusk assented. Could he have done anything else? President Johnson was in Texas recuperating from the rigors of his successful re-election campaign and would surely have paid little attention, amid such euphoria, to demands for Stevenson's dismissal or even a reprimand; so, obviously, anything Rusk might say would be ineffective. On Sunday, November 22, officials from the Legal Counsel's office and the I.O. Bureau conferred on details of the new policy. USUN officials argued that the no-voting plan was in no way a change in policy, but merely a shift in tactics arranged to permit time for negotiations. Other State Department officials, however, regarded it as far more than a tactical shift. From a policy of "firmness plus flexibility" the United States had adopted a policy which "assumes we can take the cork out of the champagne and put it back and that the fizz will still be in." In reality, the so-called tactical change undermined the strategy completely.[23]

What seems to confirm the reason for State Department irritation at the Stevenson maneuver is to be found in the President's 1964 annual report on the UN, which declares:

Shortly prior to December 1, the date for the opening of the 19th General Assembly, Soviet Foreign Minister Gromyko indicated in New York that the U.S.S.R. was prepared to make a contribution of an undisclosed amount to the United Nations to help restore its financial position.[24]

In other words, in the President's name, the State Department is offering a piece of "inside" information—existence of a Soviet fallback position—which tended to confirm the Accra report about Jacob Malik and to imply that had Stevenson not gone in for his individual brand of diplomacy, the Soviets would have accepted the "rescue fund" compromise. A senior UN official is said to have reported that Gromyko had told the then Ambassador of France, Seydoux, that the Soviets had decided to pay a part of their obligations to avoid the Article 19 crisis.

Much more could be told about this Article 19 imbroglio to demonstrate how strong was the resentment in the State Department against USUN—a resentment all the more burning because of the Department's frustration at Stevenson's immunity. In any case, the 19th General Assembly reconvened February 16 and ended February 18, 1965, without either facing the Article 19 issue or even conducting its normal business. The United States, quite understandably, was condemned on all sides for the way it had dealt with the issue. Its supporters were bitter at the United States backdown. Its opponents blamed the United States for immobilizing the Assembly at such a crucial time.

Three points may be made here:

1. USUN at no time recommended abandonment of the original Article 19 policy.

2. State Department aides in Washington concerned with Article 19 policy opposed the no-vote formula on the grounds that one rarely achieves at the conference table what cannot be held on the battlefield.

3. Stevenson's resolution of the deadlock, even though it flouted State Department policy, had to be accepted because, confronted by a determined USUN Chief, the Department lacks a damage control mechanism. History cannot concern itself with alternatives, but one could speculate what might have happened had President Kennedy been alive when faced by such flagrant disregard of policy approved by the White House.

The Article 19 case history is an example of how USUN can create *a new situation* by forcing the Department's hand, or, more specifically, how in a crisis situation, the Ambassador can overturn departmental policy with almost no fear of reprisal. No one has suggested that Stevenson's job tenure was in jeopardy at any time. Not only was Stevenson able to breach an agreed-upon policy but, what is more, he precluded any return to the original policy by this simple fact: to have repudiated Stevenson's agreement with Fedorenko might have meant Stevenson's resignation in protest, an event which not even Stevenson's worst critics in the Department would have wanted to see happen—unless the President himself had favored the resignation.

To suggest that such unilateral disregard of orders and agreements could happen once and no more is to ignore Stevenson's continuing open dissent from United States foreign policy, particularly on the Vietnam war.[25]

Notes

1. In Edward P. Doyle (ed.), *As We Knew Adlai: The Stevenson Story* (New York: Harper and Row, 1966), p. 286.

2. *Ibid.*, p. 263, Francis T. P. Plimpton writes: "In April 1961, a young CIA representative came into the then USUN gloomy offices at 2 Park Avenue and guardedly indicated to Stevenson and top USUN personnel that something was likely to happen on the shores of the erstwhile republic. The financing was to be by Cuban emigrés; no U.S. facilities were to be involved. . . . When what did happen happened, USUN was as surprised as anyone else. Stevenson accepted as true the CIA story of defecting Castro pilots bombing Castro airfields, and the CIA photography of the supposed Castro planes that had done it—which in good faith he showed to the UN General Assembly's First Committee. The disclosures that these were fakes caused him wounds over which the scar tissues never completely healed."

Pierre Salinger, *With Kennedy* (New York: Doubleday, 1966), p. 147, writes: "Governor Stevenson later told me that this had been the most 'humiliating experience' of his years in government service. He was only partially mollified by President Kennedy's explanation that the failure to inform him of the true nature of U.S. involvement in the Bay of Pigs invasion was 'a communications failure.' Stevenson felt that he had been made a fool of, and that his integrity had been seriously damaged. . . . On the Saturday [April 8, 1961], a week before the invasion [Arthur M.] Schlesinger and a top operative of the CIA went to New York and gave Stevenson a partial briefing. Stevenson later told me, however, that 'I was never told the full extent of the plan.' "

3. *Ibid.*, p. 69.

4. Theodore Sorenson, *Kennedy* (New York: Bantam, 1966), p. 322. One hears the phrase "United Nations atmosphere" a good deal in Washington in rather critical tones. One official I interviewed put it rather astringently: "Too many Mission people have been too long up there in New York. They're the tacticians for whom the ultimate reality is the Afro-Asian majority."

5. Hugh Sidey, *John F. Kennedy, President* (New York: Atheneum, 1964), pp. 57–58, describes a scene where the President thought a draft by Dean Rusk of a statement on the murder of Patrice Lumumba was too tough. "The President got Adlai Stevenson on the phone. . . . For more than an hour Kennedy and Stevenson hammered away on the statement." No doubt, the President in this case was taking the advice of one of those tacticians "for whom the ultimate reality is the Afro-Asian majority."

6. Much of what follows in this chapter is based on interviews with participant-observers, past or present, who prefer anonymity. During the latter part of Goldberg's embassy, probably 80 per cent of instructions and action proposals were prepared by Goldberg personally—for example, during the Cyprus crisis in 1967—or were initiated under his guidance in New York. Yet there are limits even for a strong personality like Goldberg. As he himself concedes, he was unable, try as he would, to budge United States policy on Vietnam until mid-1968 (after the Tet offensive in January–February 1968) as his incumbency neared its close.

7. There was little cordiality between Kennedy and Stevenson. It was always "Mr. President" and "Governor" or "Mr. Ambassador." There were few intimate social occasions between the two men. (Neither did the President call his Secretary of State "Dean," according to Sorenson, *op. cit.*, p. 303.) Interestingly, according to Arthur M. Schlesinger, Jr., when Stevenson was not present, the President referred to him as "Adlai." On page 696 of *A Thousand Days. John F. Kennedy in the White House* (New York: Houghton Mifflin, 1965), Schlesinger quotes a Kennedy telegram which begins "Dear Adlai." We can judge

how Stevenson felt about the White House from a paragraph in Doyle (ed.), *op. cit.*, p. 178, by Mary McGrory: "Some time after the Bay of Pigs, when on instructions, he had denied flatly any American complicity, I saw him as he came away from a White House meeting. 'That young man,' he said, shaking his head, 'he never says "please" and he never says "I'm sorry." ' "

8. Schlesinger, *op. cit.*, p. 410. This soft impeachment is softened even more by the author's statement that although Stevenson was invited to Cabinet and National Security Council meetings, "he was very often detained at the UN when large decisions impended at the Department or the White House. . . . To influence the making of policy it was really necessary to be in the room. . . . Cleveland and I did our best to see that the UN interest was represented in policy discussion, but we were often not in the room ourselves." It is doubtful, and Schlesinger, I believe, would agree, that "being in the room" when some fateful decision was being made would have wrought much change. Schlesinger has noted in an interview with me (March 4, 1967) that "policy is set at the early meetings, the preliminary meetings and then it's too late to change direction." There was little of moment going on at the UN during the fateful days when the Bay of Pigs crisis was in the making, and Stevenson could have been "in the room" via the shuttle plane in two hours while policy was being made. With regard to adequate briefing on the operation itself by those who were "in the room," Schlesinger writes (*ibid.*, p. 244): "In preparation for the [UN] debate, Tracy Barnes [CIA] and I had a long talk with Stevenson April 8 [1961]. But our briefing, *which was probably unduly vague*, left Stevenson with the impression that no action would take place during the UN discussion of the Cuban item." (Emphasis added.)

9. Stewart Alsop and Charles Bartlett, "In Time of Crisis," *Saturday Evening Post* (December 8, 1962), p. 15. "There is disagreement in retrospect about what Stevenson really wanted. 'Adlai wanted a Munich,' says a non-admiring official who learned of his proposal. 'He wanted to trade the Turkish, Italian and British missile bases for the Cuban bases.' " So wrote the *Post* authors. *Newsweek* (December 17, 1962), p. 17, said "the article pictured Stevenson as a sort of Neville Chamberlain." In the same issue, *Newsweek* (p. 17) said that President Kennedy had approved of a crisis piece, had okayed Bartlett and Alsop as authors, and had told his White House staff to ask the "EXCOM" (Executive Committee of the National Security Council) "to cooperate within the bounds of security requirements." Bartlett was described as a close friend of the President. Of especial interest is a column in the same issue (p. 28) by Kenneth G. Crawford, a very well-informed

Washington correspondent, who said that a widely circulated theory that the President wanted to rid himself of Stevenson "was more or less supported by the failure of the White House in two reaffirmations of the President's confidence in Stevenson, to repudiate the Bartlett-Alsop version of events leading up to the decisions to set up a naval blockade of Cuba."

10. The USUN, according to well-placed informants, received five thousand pieces of mail and numerous editorials, mostly favorable to Stevenson. Said another Stevenson friend: "Adlai had a constituency and the Administration couldn't ditch him thereafter. The article had actually strengthened his position; he was a power in the Democratic Party and with the American people. The Administration realized that they needed Adlai—after all, Kennedy had only won by 7/10 of 1 per cent over Nixon—and his role in future policy-making was strengthened and his views were taken more into account. But Adlai was too gentlemanly and he didn't inject himself into policy-making any more than he had before."

11. Elie Abel, *The Missile Crisis* (New York: Bantam, 1966), pp. 79–80. This book is regarded as a highly authentic report. The author had access to many confidential documents and interviews with high Administration officials whom he quotes freely. For a Stevenson view of the crisis, see Murray Kempton in *London Spectator* (December 28, 1962), p. 981. See note 14 below.

12. Stevenson was a victim of selective "leakage." Nothing was leaked at the time or thereafter about Defense Secretary McNamara's casualness about the missile crisis. Roger Hilsman quotes McNamara as saying: "A missile is a missile. It makes no great difference whether you are killed by a missile fired from the Soviet Union or from Cuba." In other words, says Hilsman, who was "in the room" a good deal of the time, "the clear implication of McNamara's position was that the United States should do nothing, but simply accept the presence of Soviet missiles in Cuba and sit tight." (*To Move a Nation* [New York: Doubleday, 1967], p. 195.) President Kennedy and other Administration advisers disagreed with McNamara's placid view. The Kennedy crisis speech October 22, 1962, in fact, was an implied criticism of McNamara's view: "Nuclear weapons are so destructive, and ballistic missiles are so swift, that any substantially increased possibility of their use or any sudden change in their deployment may well be regarded as a definite threat to the peace." (*New York Times*, October 23, 1962.) Despite what would seem to be a monumental misjudgment by McNamara, no criticism was ever "leaked" about him.

13. Among Stevenson's friends, there is a dispute as to whether he suggested McCloy or it was suggested to him. The true story, I believe, is that the suggestion for McCloy (who was in Germany on private business during this time) came from General Lucius D. Clay, a leading Republican, with whom President Kennedy was in fairly constant communication during the crisis week. It was General Clay who over the phone Monday, October 22, 1962, suggested McCloy to the President as someone who could "back up those panty-waists you have over at the UN." To ease things for Stevenson, he was given a choice: Phleger, a colorless, uninfluential Western Republican, or McCloy, his very antithesis. Naturally, Stevenson chose McCloy, and this led Stevenson's friends to believe that it was he who had chosen McCloy.

14. In his 1500-word *London Spectator* dispatch datelined United Nations, N.Y., Kempton quoted Stevenson as saying, "Mr. Kennedy, *at our insistence,* has been closer to the United Nations than any President before him. . . . We have kept the Administration's nose to the line on the Congo." (Emphasis in original.)

15. Not too much is known about the controversy from the Stevenson side because John Bartlow Martin, his official biographer, who has the bulk of the Stevenson papers, says he is contractually barred from disclosing them to anybody. However, he told me a good section of the biography will be devoted to Article 19. Several friends of Stevenson who worked with him at USUN were unavailable for interviews. My sources are neither pro- nor anti-Stevenson. The material on which I have based my report has been viewed by high government officials. Where possible I have tried to confirm the material by objective information, such as dates or places. This report is in no way the last word and can only wait until the evidence or documentation can be thoroughly examined.

16. United Nations, Statement on the Collection of Contributions as of June 30, 1964 (UN Document ST/ADM/SET. 8/189, July 15, 1964), p. 4.

17. For a summary of the resolution see United Nations *General Assembly Resolution No. 1731* (XVI), December 20, 1961.

18. The sources for these and subsequent statements are confidential.

19. United Nations, *General Assembly Resolution No. 1854 B* (XVII), December 19, 1962.

20. U.S. President, 1964—(Johnson), *U.S. Participation in the United Nations:* Report by the President to Congress for 1964, pp. 2 ff.

21. It should be noted that President Johnson was in the middle of his election campaign against Senator Goldwater.

22. Department of State Bulletin (November 9, 1964), p. 681: "Letter from U.S. Representative Adlai Stevenson to Secretary-General and text of memorandum, letter of transmittal, October 8, 1964."

23. As an indication of the feeling between State and USUN during this period, one official said: "In fairness to Stevenson, it may be said, that he was the victim of poor advice on tactics from one or more of his political staff at the Mission. In 1964, he was an old, broken man, tired and no longer the old Adlai. He couldn't play the poker game and he wavered under the pressure, became indecisive and confused. He convinced himself with the advice of his New York staff that the no-voting procedure was the way out. It was not something done with malice by Stevenson."

24. U.S. President, 1964—(Johnson), *op. cit.*, p. 7.

25. Perhaps the misunderstanding as to the nature of the USUN post began even before Stevenson's appointment. Joseph E. Johnson, president of the Carnegie Endowment for International Peace, saw Stevenson shortly after it was reported that President Kennedy had offered him the USUN mission. An expert in UN-USUN-State relationships, Johnson urged Stevenson to be sure that the Assistant Secretary of State in charge of international organization would be someone with whom Stevenson could work since many of the instructions to USUN would in fact be written by the Assistant Secretary. Stevenson replied: "I don't see why that should be. I don't see why there cannot be in effect two men in charge of foreign affairs. After all, the British have a Foreign Minister and a Minister for Commonwealth Affairs." Johnson pointed out that the two ministries "deal with different countries, not the same ones." (Private communication from Johnson to the author, Feb. 1, 1968.)

10/ Arthur J. Goldberg

> The best instrument of a Government
> wishing to persuade another Govern-
> ment will always remain the spoken
> words of a decent man.
>
> JULES CAMBON[1]

Since UN diplomacy has become parliamentary, multilateral, popular, and public, it is evident that the USUN
Chief must be a personage whose resources also include
the kind of status which brings prestige to a President in
the execution of national foreign policy. He must be able
enough so that the end result of this particular kind of
diplomacy—the vote—is in favor of American policy.[2]
His reputation must be such as to conform to the idea
proposed by Inis L. Claude, Jr., that the UN is an adapta-
tion of the welfare state philosophy to the realm of world
affairs. In an organization where the majority of nations
are poor and disadvantaged, an American spokesman
should probably have as a resource a known involvement

with social concerns, with liberalism, and a record of having articulated great social issues.

The (sixth) USUN Chief, Arthur J. Goldberg, had that reputation because of his labor movement background and his Supreme Court avant-gardism. In addition he had another great advantage, his relationship to the President. He once told a press conference:

> *I exacted only one commitment from the President of the United States when he asked me to take this post and that commitment was this: "I would like to have you hear my voice. I would like to express frankly and candidly to you my opinions about the various issues that I have to deal with here at the United Nations. . . ."*
>
> *I will tell you, frankly, after months in this office that I have had frequent and free access to the President of the United States. I will say with all equal candor that my voice has been heard—and that is all I asked for. That commitment has been honored by the President of the United States.[3]*

When Ambassador Goldberg resigned from the Supreme Court he signaled something far more important than his reputed dysphoria on the bench.[4] He was letting it be known that the United States Mission had become a major job in the federal establishment. A man of long experience in and out of government, Goldberg had been Secretary of Labor some twenty months when he was appointed by President Kennedy to the Supreme Court, August 29, 1962. After Robert Kennedy's resignation as Attorney-General, President Johnson unsuccessfully urged the post on Goldberg. In accepting the USUN post,

Goldberg surrendered a lifetime appointment as an Associate Justice July 28, 1965, at a considerable drop in salary—an indication that the job has become tremendously attractive to ambitious men. If the position leads nowhere up, at least the USUN Chief's superior, the Secretary of State, may suffer the same difficulty without the warm, compensating glow of personal publicity.[5]

In his UN appointments, a President is faced and will continue to be faced by a dilemma. If, after Goldberg's retirement, he had appointed a career diplomat, even one of great stature, it would have been regarded as a downgrading of the post. Yet to appoint someone blessed with his own constituency, like Adlai Stevenson, or with ranking governmental accreditations, like Goldberg and Ball, means setting up a little State Department all on its own and thus encouraging even further the aggregative, diffusive, polycentric nature of the American foreign policy process. President Johnson clearly followed precedent after Stevenson's death by appointing a figure of some national distinction. From the first day of the oath-taking ceremony at the White House he aided Goldberg in every way to strengthen his UN position.[6] What quickly became clear to UN delegations was expressed by *The New York Times*: "Stevenson, though enormously admired by his colleagues, was merely the representative of the United States; Arthur Goldberg is the representative of Lyndon Johnson."[7]

Perhaps of more interest is that Goldberg has had a particular status in the party-in-the-government and the party-in-the-electorate in contrast to Stevenson, who, while important in the party-in-the-electorate, rated low, under both Presidents Johnson and Kennedy, in the party-in-the government. From the standpoint of the party-in-the-government, Stevenson was a lame duck, but not within the party-in-the-electorate. There his status was much higher than that of Ambassador Goldberg. Ambassador Austin had little status in either of the two party concepts referred to above, since as a Republican he could have little significance among Democrats. What he represented to President Truman and the party-in-the-government was insurance—insurance against partisan attacks in Congress in the same way that Henry L. Stimson and Frank Knox were intended as insurance for President Roosevelt. Ambassador Lodge had status in the party-in-the-government, but, as it turned out, not enough in the party-in-the-electorate. It may be rather paradoxical to suggest that, unlike his three predecessors, each of whom ran successfully for some public office, Goldberg should have status in *both* party concepts even though he has yet to run for anything at the polls. Yet the fact that he has not run for anything may be the very reason for his domestic political strength. Second, the fact that he has not indicated any public interest in elective office maintains the image of an above-the-battle American diplomat whose ambitions transcend domestic politics.

Goldberg has been given high marks by some UN correspondents for his handling of a number of issues.[8] They have noted that he has been skillful in avoiding domestic political issues and in not allowing himself to be used by pressure groups, either of which would have created embarrassments for him at the UN.[9]

Goldberg feels that among the changes he helped to produce at the UN, one of the most important has been the restoration of the Security Council as a "negotiating body and not a debating society." As he expressed it to me during an interview:

> *In the old days, there were lots of speeches, votes, and vetoes. The change dates from the Kashmir war between India and Pakistan. There I inaugurated a policy of debate, yes, but also consultation and negotiation. After all, the Security Council is a political instrumentality. Negotiation is a painstaking process. If that can't be undertaken, I've said, "wash it out," knock off the debate and the issue and let's turn to something else.*

An example of USUN Chief–UN influence on foreign policy when the Mission is headed by a strong personality with his own high bargaining power was reported in *The New York Times* by Graham Hovey, member of the *Times* editorial board who specializes in African affairs. The article dealt with the United States draft resolution on Southwest Africa, which declared that South Africa "forfeits all rights to continue to administer the territory."[10] Hovey wrote:

> *Some members of the American delegation regard the "action proposal" that Arthur J. Goldberg presented to the*

General Assembly as his most significant achievement in 15 months as United States Representative to the UN. It should at least dilute rumors that Ambassador Goldberg finds himself only an errand boy at the U.N. For President Johnson and Secretary of State Rusk . . . the Southwest African proposal was largely the creation of Mr. Goldberg and the delegation, not a finished policy sent up from Washington. . . . It can be doubted that State on its own would have produced so bold a document.[11]

The post-October 27 developments on Southwest Africa, most notably the 5th Special Session of the General Assembly which convened April 21, 1967, have raised questions as to the extent of the influence exercised by the USUN on the policy process. Some observers feel that Charles W. Engelhard, Jr., a close friend of President Johnson and Vice-President Hubert H. Humphrey, has far greater influence on United States-South African relations than State Department officials in Washington or at the USUN. An exceedingly wealthy American with huge investments in South Africa, Engelhard is regarded as a significant interest group all by himself.[12] A study of where he was during the weeks of bargaining between State and USUN preceding the UN vote would be a valuable piece of research into the workings of pressure groups. It is known that the African desk of the State Department and the USUN worked together closely to support the resolution despite the reluctance of the "Seventh Floor" (as the State Department executive domain is described) to engage in such action.

There was a belief—the result of a kind of euphoria

which descends over the UN delegates when an anti-colonial resolution is passed with near unanimity—that the United States would immediately step in and virtually order out the militia. This has so far failed to materialize. Although the USUN has favored "peaceful dialogue" with South Africa rather than force, "New York" has also favored greater pressure on the Vorster government than Undersecretaries of State Eugene V. Rostow and Nicholas Katzenbach would find tolerable. We may have had a scenario based on these considerations:

1. The African world is bitterly disappointed at the World Court rejection of petitioners' claims against the Southwest Africa mandate.

2. The Asian-African bloc, some Latin American states, some West European and, of course, the Communist bloc have the votes to overturn the Court's decision that the petitioners had no standing in the case.

3. The USUN decides that the United States should not stand with Britain or France, who are planning to abstain on a resolution.

4. Therefore go along with a resolution acceptable to all sides.[18]

In a sense this is a strategy which keeps South Africa as the villain and the United States in at least an ambiguous role as to action, an unambiguous role as to rhetoric. Would it have turned out differently had there been no USUN or influential USUN Chief? My guess is that, first, without the UN forum the South African issue would be without the moral meaning it has developed over twenty years; second, with the UN anticolonial majority comprising at least two-thirds of the membership, a superpower like the United States must think twice before choosing sides, particularly on as touchy an issue as colonialism *cum* racism; third, a USUN which over the years has been sensitized to such issues at the UN will find it impossible not to side with the majority, while at the same time it will seek to ensure that the cost of siding with that majority does not involve the United States in adventures which may, domestically, be too costly.[14] But in the UN atmosphere of what I would call cyclical diplomacy—the annual submission of old issues (representation of China or Korea, for example) for discussion and vote with the certainty that they will come up at a subsequent session—Southwest Africa is bound to appear again and again. On each occasion a decision will need to be made, even though the pace at which the issue moves is reminiscent of Zeno's paradox. With the cyclical approach, one may expect that no threat of force will be realized. Should there be another Sharpeville massacre in South Africa or some similar outbreak of violence, the bargaining process between State and USUN would become, necessarily, more intense because of the UN pressure. In the words of Adlai Stevenson in the *London Spectator*, another USUN Chief would attempt "to keep the Administration's nose on the UN line."

Ambassador Goldberg enjoyed a special kind of tactical

freedom necessitated by the doubling of UN membership since the days of Ambassadors Austin or Lodge.[15] On the other hand, he did not always exercise the same sway over policy and decision-making as did Lodge during his years of service. Or perhaps one should say that compared to the UN of a decade or more ago, the present UN with its 124 members (as of May 1968) has brought many more actors into the various subsystems so that Lodge's one-upmanship during the Dulles reign at the State Department could not work today.

One period in the USUN history which may have prefigured the present pattern of the USUN has received little attention. I refer to the Austin-Gross period, during much of which Ernest A. Gross was a prominent figure as Deputy Ambassador and frequently acting Ambassador during Austin's illnesses.

Notes

1. Jules Cambon, *The Diplomatist* (London: Philip Allan, 1931). Quoted in Herbert C. Kelman (ed.), *International Behavior* (New York: Holt, Rinehart and Winston, 1965), p. 523.

2. I do not mean to overemphasize the vote. In its affirmative sense, the result may mean very little; say, a UN resolution which might call for use of force against South Africa. Yet it would be difficult for an American President to accept—if only from the standpoint of his own political prestige—continuing defeats at the UN reported regularly in the American press.

3. Press release No. 4779, *U.S. Mission to the UN* (December 22,

1965), press conference transcript at close of 20th General Assembly session, p. 5.

4. Only four Supreme Court justices have resigned during this century for reasons other than those of health—Hughes, Clarke, Byrnes, and Goldberg. "In terms of prestige and socio-political status American Supreme Court justices are an elite group who enjoy the very pinnacle of public esteem and probably they outrank the President most (if not all) of the time." Glendon Schubert, in Lewis Edinger (ed.), *Political Leadership in Industrial Societies* (New York: John Wiley and Sons, 1967), p. 232, note 23.

5. Don K. Price (ed., for the American Assembly, Columbia University), *The Secretary of State* (Englewood Cliffs, N.J.: Prentice-Hall, 1960), p. 1: "The first Secretary of State of the United States of America, Thomas Jefferson, became President. Each of the next three Presidents—Madison, Monroe and John Quincy Adams—had also served as Secretary of State. Since then, however, that position has been no road to political advancement, even though it has retained by tradition the highest rank in the Cabinet. Indeed, in recent years the Secretary of State has seemed to be the official scapegoat for a nation which resents the sacrifices of two world wars and the frustration of the idealistic hopes which carried it to victory but failed to establish a firm basis for peace." (See, above, Chapter 8, note 18.) Price's history is not quite correct. Secretary of State Martin Van Buren (1829–1831) was elected Vice-President in 1832 and President in 1836. Secretary of State James Buchanan (1845–1849) was elected President in 1856. Secretary of State Charles Evans Hughes became Chief Justice of the Supreme Court in 1930, having served under two Presidents from 1921 to 1925. Nevertheless there is a good measure of truth in the Price assessment, although from the standpoint of upward political mobility it is not such a dead end as the office of New York City Mayor or the British Secretary of State for the Colonies.

6. On November 29, 1966, President Johnson opened a new office to be used when he stayed at his Texas ranch. The following press colloquy took place: "Q. Could you tell us generally, Mr. President, just so to speak in honor of the occasion of using this new office, what were you working on today? A. I signed a good deal of correspondence, and there are several matters here. . . . Here are some matters from Ambassador Goldberg that I have not had a chance to read and digest and get to the bottom of." (*New York Times*, November 30, 1966.) On May 3, 1967, at a White House press conference, President Johnson said, "I am meeting momentarily with the [National] Security Council and Ambassador Goldberg. We will review various alternatives in the

United Nations on the diplomatic front and the military front." (*Ibid.*, May 4, 1967.) In these two cases, it is the President himself who has given Ambassador Goldberg publicly an extraordinary kind of status: the publicly acknowledged right to communicate directly with the President or the impression that he has that right, and, second, that he is a full participant within the NSC not only on UN and diplomatic matters but also on military problems. (See Chapter 1, note 19.) It is quite an advantage when a government official can have direct access of this kind to the Chief Executive because it could mean enhancement of influence on foreign policy. "[Harry] Hopkins' reports went directly to the President—on the basis of speed alone a decided advantage." ("Special Diplomatic Agents of the President," *Annals of the American Academy*, CCCVII [September 1956], 132.)

7. *New York Times Sunday Magazine* (February 6, 1966), p. 16.

8. Louis B. Fleming, Los Angeles *Times-Mirror* (July 17, 1966), credited Goldberg with a number of achievements: pressing for an American policy change toward Rhodesia following its November 1965 unilateral declaration of independence; restoring the Mission "to a new level of efficiency"; becoming the first really full-time ambassador to the UN; "master-minding" negotiations for the India-Pakistan ceasefire. Goldberg has been given credit by Clayton Fritchey ("Our Heroes at the U.N.," *Harper's Magazine* [February 1967], p. 36), for "his one and only victory over Rusk," namely, settlement of the Article 19 dispute. Actually the compromise with the Soviet Union had been arranged long before Goldberg took office. In fact, it would have been announced by President Johnson at the twentieth anniversary celebration of the UN's founding in San Francisco. However, the speech was leaked to James Reston of *The New York Times*, who wrote (June 23, 1965, p. 40) that "It is reported he [Johnson] will try not only to end the dispute over compulsory payments for the U.N. military operations by suggesting that these payments be voluntary in the future but that he will offer to increase U.S. contributions to the U.N.'s technical assistance and development fund." When the President saw the Reston column, he ordered the speech rewritten. Thus it was left to Goldberg to finally "settle" what in fact had been settled weeks before. Goldberg's contribution to the Article 19 settlement was to persuade ex-President Eisenhower, who was preparing to attack the proposed agreement, not to do so and to mute what might have been a full-scale attack by Congress on the settlement.

9. Prior to his USUN appointment, Justice Goldberg was known as a Zionist and a close friend of Israeli leaders. The night of President

Kennedy's departure on his first European trip, Goldberg, then Secretary of Labor, arranged a meeting in the President's Waldorf-Astoria suite with David Ben Gurion, then visiting New York. (Goldberg was a good enough friend of Ben Gurion to suggest that he give the President a chance to say a few words, since the former Israeli Prime Minister was a well-known conversational monopolist.) Yet neither his admiration of Israel nor what might have seemed like other occupational disabilities for diplomacy played any significant role during the Middle East debates at the UN in June–July 1967 except for some *ad hominem* attacks by the Syrian Ambassador to the UN. However, unconfirmed reports at the UN said that President Johnson had expressed doubts that Goldberg ought to present the United States Middle East policy statement. This was meant to explain why President Johnson made the presentation himself in Washington, on the morning of June 19, 1967, several hours before the opening of the UN Assembly emergency session. Actually Goldberg had urged the President himself to deliver the United States policy declaration at the session in New York as Premier Kosygin planned to do. President Johnson agreed to make the speech but not at the UN. (It was made before an educators' conference at the State Department.) Ever since his speech at San Francisco (see note 8, above), which was poorly received by UN delegates, Johnson avoided speech-making at the UN.

10. *The New York Times* (October 17, 1966). The final resolution passed by the UN General Assembly on October 27, 1966, followed quite closely the United States resolution, although later interpretations over certain phrases led to clashes between African countries and the Western bloc. The UN resolution is GA/2145 (XXI) and is referred to above, Chapter 1, note 19.

11. "The apogee of his career at the UN" is the phrase used by Drew Middleton in *The New York Times* to describe Goldberg's behind-the-scenes negotiations with Soviet Foreign Minister Gromyko and Soviet Ambassador Dobrynin during the Middle East crisis in 1967. (*The New York Times*, July 26, 1967.) Another example of Goldberg-UN "public relations" influence on the White House occurred April 4, 1968. Having flown to St. Patrick's Cathedral for the investiture of Archbishop Terence J. Cooke, the President delayed his return trip to Washington at Goldberg's suggestion for an impromptu visit with Thant at the UN Secretariat building. "White House aides said that Mr. Johnson had made a sudden decision to visit Mr. Thant on Mr. Goldberg's suggestion. The White House aides said Mr. Goldberg had made the suggestion when he met Mr. Johnson at the cathedral earlier in the afternoon.

'Mr. Goldberg said if he could fit it into his schedule, it would be a good idea.' " (*The New York Times*, April 5, 1968.) The full story is even more interesting as a reflection of President Johnson's interest in the UN. On leaving the cathedral, Goldberg was unable to find his limousine. He decided to walk back to his office, eleven blocks away. Upon his arrival at USUN headquarters, he was told that the President had been trying to get him on the phone from the Central Park helicopter pad for the past quarter-hour. Goldberg phoned back and was told the President was ready to go to the UN if Thant was available. While a Presidential aide waited on one phone, Goldberg arranged the Thant-Johnson meeting on another.

12. "A Special Report on American Involvement in the South African Economy," *Africa Today* (January 1966), p. 27–29, deals with Engelhard. *Forbes*, August 1, 1965, did a cover story on him.

13. Johannesburg *Sunday Times*, April 2, 1967, said that "when the resolution was proposed last autumn, the phrase 'practical means' was inserted as a piece of deliberate ambiguity to secure passage of the resolution. As one Washington expert put it, 'The United Nations resolution is policy-concealing rather than decision-making. The phrase conceals the vast gulf between the United States, Britain, and France on the one side, and most of the Afro-Asian bloc on the other.' " (Dispatch by the author.)

14. In his address to the General Assembly, April 26, 1967, Ambassador Goldberg introduced a new "actor" in the USUN–State Department subsystem, American public opinion: "I do know that public opinion in my country, and indeed in many parts of the world, would not understand a policy which seems ready to resort to immediate coercion rather than explore the possibilities of peaceful progress." (Statement by Ambassador Goldberg in Plenary Session on the Question of South West Africa, USUN *Press Release* 49 (April 26, 1967), p. 4.)

15. One freedom he does not enjoy is an immunity from backbiting by other members of the Presidential entourage. It is apparently an occupational hazard of USUN Chiefs. A powerful New York political figure, quite close to President Johnson, during the winter of 1966–1967 opened an anti-Goldberg drive accusing the Ambassador behind his back of disloyalty to Administration policy on Vietnam. No evidence to bolster the accusation was offered.

11/ The Early Days

Ernest A. Gross was legal adviser to the State Department from August 15, 1947, until February 14, 1949, when he was named Assistant Secretary for Congressional Relations. During his term as Assistant Secretary he negotiated passage of amendments to the 1945 Participation Act which provided for *The* Deputy Representative to the United Nations, a title and status which meant that the holder of the position would be a genuine second-in-command.

In an interview at his home Gross told me:

I was interested in the job's potentialities. I had no particular sense of a government career, no desire for one. My real ambition had always been to go up to the UN. When I told [Secretary of State Dean] Acheson I wanted the UN job, he practically ordered me to go to a psychiatrist, in friendly fashion. He thought I ought to have my head examined for wanting the UN job.

As early as 1949, a young lawyer was looking to the USUN, rather than to the State Department itself, for a career in diplomacy. And it was during this period that the USUN began to demonstrate its hunger for a life of its own and freedom from too much State Department control. Gross demonstrated this desire on colonial issues, most notably on North Africa when he indicated publicly his disagreement with State Department support of the French position in Tunisia and Morocco. This point was reached April 10, 1950, when the Security Council was considering inscription of the question of Tunisian independence on its agenda. Gross, who favored the item's inscription, was bound by State Department instructions calling for abstention. These instructions were incorporated in a speech sent to him from Washington.

Gross did only one thing to the speech. He added a sentence at the beginning, without obtaining prior State Department approval. He opened his State Department-approved declaration before the Security Council with these eleven words:

[Mr. President,] I express the following views of my government on this subject.[1]

UN newspaper correspondents had no difficulty in interpreting the meaning of Gross's sentence and so reported.[2] Gross described the scene which followed:

After I read that opening sentence, from that point on it didn't matter what I said. The blunt tone of that sentence was enough. On the record nothing could be held against me by Washington because I had said what I was supposed to say. But when the Security Council recessed, I was surrounded in the Delegates' Lounge by a group of Asians and the small number of Africans then in the UN. They shook my hand and they were so pleased. What I had done was to make it possible to continue the dialogue.

The aftermath was that he was called down to Washington by John Hickerson, then Assistant Secretary for International Organization Affairs. Gross had already been lectured by Secretary Acheson about North Africa and had been told that relations with France were the "lodestar" of American foreign policy and therefore the United States could not play "UN politics." In Washington he was given anew the full background of United States-French problems on colonial issues and the extent to which these issues were a big domestic political problem for the French government. Gross said:

What triggered this particular confrontation with the European desk [of the State Department] and with Acheson and [George] Kennan was that I had not given sufficient weight to the U.S.-France relationship nor taken account of the French domestic situation, that the battle in France was between the moderates on one side and the army and colonial administration on the other, that the latter were exercising more influence than the Quai d'Orsay. However, the people in the African section of State were not unhappy at what I'd done. *[Emphasis added.]*[3]

179

The "Other" State Department

The USUN "autonomy" is a matter not only of degree but of kind, not merely quantitative but also qualitative. For example, said Gross, the USUN Chief can commit his government as no other ambassador can. If the United States representative to the Security Council votes for a resolution against Washington instructions, there is no reconsideration. He voted for it, and it would be a legal and constitutional commitment. Realistically, of course, it would be another matter whether Congress or the President would accept such a decision. No other ambassador has the power to commit the United States like the USUN Chief, because, says Gross, the USUN lives by the UN Charter, which is different from the founding documents of NATO or the OAS.

The USUN Chief benefits from what Gross calls "influence-breeding exposure." By this he means that the post is one which creates high influence because of the incumbent's continuing interaction with various formal, official, as well as private and unofficial, groups and interests. In a sense the USUN Chief is our ambassador to the Secretary-General, which is a sort of "political Vatican touch." Gross said:

The Secretary-General has no more troops than has the Pope, but there is in that relationship something which rubs off on the USUN Chief. When you get an activist, dynamic S-G, like Trygve Lie and Hammarskjöld, he makes the United States Ambassador active and dynamic. In time of crisis, the S-G's views and actions are as important a political phenomenon as the Pope in Rome and his views.

Gross regards the real importance of the UN, and therefore the USUN, as arising from a new balance-of-power concept which stems from (a) the nuclear deadlock, (b) the polycentric nature of the Communist movement today, (c) the therefore heightened importance of the smaller states because the superpowers are competing for their allegiance.

A second but important aspect of the UN is the nature of its forum which provides for discussion and debate, for dramatizing and recording agreements, tacit or otherwise. As an example of the "nature of the forum" idea, Gross offered the following example.[4]

When the Security Council meeting at Lake Success ended on the afternoon of July 25, 1950, Sir Benegal Rau, the Indian representative, asked Gross to step across the corridor from the Council chamber into an empty room to discuss a problem. Sir Benegal said he was worried about threats to Yugoslavia from "Cominform countries," particularly propaganda in Soviet and satellite countries accusing Yugoslavia of preparing for aggression with American support. Sir Benegal said that he was expressing a personal view (throughout the interview he repeated that it was all his personal view) in suggesting that the Security Council ought to send an observer group or mission to Yugoslavia to see and report as to whether Yugoslavia was actually preparing for aggression.[5]

Gross said he, too, would speak personally and asked whether Sir Benegal would consider the desirability of the Security Council's creating a group or commission with

authority on its own determination to visit or send observation teams to any area threatened with aggression or
military hostilities. Such a commission could go not only
to Yugoslavia but also to Formosa, Iran, Berlin, or other
hot spots. Out of this "personal" conversation was born
the Peace Observation Commission, of which the United
States and the USSR were members.[6]

The story portrays quite vividly the unusual role which
the UN had begun to develop as early as 1950. Since a
large number of diplomats are at the UN in constant,
almost daily contact with each other on a large number of
issues and are able to meet regularly at a specific place, no
question is irrelevant to raise nor is anything too pointed,
as it might be in a different diplomatic context or atmosphere. Sir Benegal could in his indirect and "personal"
style bring up Yugoslavia's concern over Russia without
the action having the overpowering significance it might
have had, were it presented in a conference by appointment after discussion by two Foreign Offices. Sir Benegal
could say he was speaking personally, not having yet
consulted his government, and it would not be im-
plausible, but rather quite appropriate in the UN forum.
It would have been difficult for Sir Benegal to have called
upon the Secretary of State to discuss "my own idea"
when there was a colleague at the UN with whom he was
in constant association and with whom he could open
a conversation with "by the way." Gross explained this
aspect of UN atmosphere in relation to USUN function:

The important part of multilateral diplomacy, as a technique in diplomacy as against the traditional diplomatists and their functioning, is just this—that you can have a casualness about an important issue. It's a new way of carrying on the old-fashioned diplomacy. Without this multilateral technique and constant contact, the Indian government would have had to make a formal démarche to the U.S. and it would have meant intergovernmental consultations which India didn't want. There was no intergovernmental flapping. I could offer my own ideas, as my personal ideas, without the need for departmental consulting.

Why could not the Indian Ambassador in London have taken up the matter with the American Ambassador in London?

It would have been out of context for those two to deal with such a topic, whereas it was within the context of the Security Council, and we were dealing with some similar particular problem and we could take it up in the UN even though Belgrade was unwilling to approach the U.S. directly.

Gross also raised the notion that other United States embassies must accomplish certain tasks if the USUN is to perform successfully. He offered this example: In 1950, the USSR introduced a motion in the Security Council to invite the Chinese Communists to present their case against American aggression on Formosa. The United States lost by one vote. The motion passed because the United States, favoring an open forum for the Council, declined to define its negative vote as a veto. If better groundwork had been done by the United States Embassy in Ecuador, it is quite probable that the vote of Ecuador (then a nonpermanent Council member) would have been cast in favor of the United States position.[7] "This is the important relationship between bilateral and multilateral diplomacy; the missions in the field must also do their work if we are to succeed at the UN table," he told me.

The informal nature of the UN subsystem is seen in an unusual meeting which attracted almost no attention in the press or other media several days after the outbreak of the Korean war. The meeting, between Gross, Jacob Malik, and Secretary-General Trygve Lie, was out in the open, a luncheon given by the Soviet Assistant Secretary-General for Security Council Affairs, Constantin Zinchenko, at the Stockholm Restaurant on Long Island. The Soviet boycott of the Security Council was then in its fifth month, having begun January 13, 1950. Lie was seated between Gross and Malik.[8]

From confidential sources and records I have reconstructed the conversation which took place June 27, 1950: Malik criticized Lie's attitude on Korea as "one-sided" just like the Security Council action June 25, 1950, and argued that the Security Council decision was illegal because of the Soviet absence and the absence of the Chinese mainland representative. He charged that American planes were bombing Korean cities and people. His luncheon companions denied the charge, arguing that the United States was acting in aid of a Council resolution to repel an unlawful invasion. Lie asked about the suggestion for appointment of a mediator. Gross said the precondition for any mediatory or other procedure was cessation of hostilities and withdrawal of North Korean forces. Lie agreed. Malik made no comment. The Secretary-General then invited the Soviet delegate to return with them after lunch to the Security Council meeting that afternoon. It was on June 27 that the second resolution setting up the Korean operation was to be voted on, and had the Russian returned and vetoed, "he would have buggered up everything," said Gross. "I had a good enough relationship with Lie to bawl the pants off him."[9]

Here we have an example of interaction among three subsystems—UN, USUN, Soviet—which are part of an over-all international subsystem during what David Easton might call "a stressful disturbance on the system."[10] Three actors were involved at the Stockholm Restaurant for some two hours during which a series of transactions moved across the boundary separating one subsystem from another in the form of an output-input relationship. In this instance, the output-input linkage did not immediately lead to any exchange, probably because it was too soon—barely three days after the outbreak of hostilities—for either of the two antagonists to feel that the personal contact at the luncheon table could extend to some mutually beneficial relationship, such as settlement of the war.

Application of systems analysis in the absence of publishable transactional documentation would seem impossible since it would be difficult without it to analyze the following Eastonian variables: nature of inputs, variable conditions under which they constitute a stressful disturbance on the system, environmental and systemic conditions that generate such stressful conditions, typical ways in which systems have sought to cope with stress, role of information feedback, and the part that outputs play in these conversion and coping processes.

Nevertheless, what we have here is a case study of a "trialogue" with some quotable material from two of three sources—the UN Secretary-General and the acting USUN Chief—and the possibility of attempting systems analysis when more material is available.

Notes

1. *USUN Press Release 1461*, April 10, 1952, Statement by Ambassador Ernest A. Gross, Deputy United States Representative, before the Security Council on Tunisia.

2. *The New York Times*, April 15, 1952, said that "Ernest A. Gross . . . in announcing the abstention of the United States last week made it plain that he was only expressing the instructions he had received from the State Department."

3. I have emphasized the closing sentence because it is reminiscent of a similar reaction some years later by the "African section of State" described in Chapter 9, note 4. The regional or area desks of State can themselves be important actors in the subsystem of USUN as well as State.

4. I have, on a confidential basis, studied documents relating to this case history.

5. During this time, the Yugoslav government was so frightened of a Soviet attack that it had opened a "peace offensive" against Moscow by seeking to enlist Western liberals in visits to Yugoslav frontiers. How serious this was to Yugoslavia was noted in 1952 when then Foreign Minister Edward Kardelj and Yugoslav Ambassador Ales Bebler met with emissaries of the American Federation of Labor at the Yugoslav Embassy on Fifth Avenue and urged that a three-man team consisting of William Green, George Meany, and David Dubinsky tour the Yugoslav frontier and report publicly whether they had seen any signs of Yugoslav preparations for aggression against its Cominform neighbors. Nothing ever came of this idea. This story is known personally to the writer.

6. *New York Times Sunday Magazine* (September 21, 1958), p. 70, by Ernest A. Gross: "Later that same year [1950] the 14-member U.N. Peace Observation Commission was organized as a permanent body to 'observe and report' upon the request of the General Assembly or the Security Council in any area of dangerous international tension."

7. United Nations, Security Council, 506th Meeting, September 29, 1950, Complaint: *Armed Invasion Taiwan*, p. 359.

8. Trygve Lie, *In the Cause of Peace* (New York: Macmillan, 1954), p. 332, omits a good deal of that discussion between the American and Soviet representatives.

9. The Goldberg embassy, it is believed in some UN circles, led to the return of Ambassador Malik as Fedorenko's replacement. It is known that Goldberg did not relish Fedorenko's "hard line" approach to United States-Soviet relations. Malik is a veteran "peace" negotiator—involved with ending the Berlin blockade and with the preliminary meetings which led to the Korean armistice. In addition, he seems to get along better with UN colleagues, including Goldberg, than did Fedorenko. Relations between Malik and Goldberg were friendly but tough. At a private luncheon at the Soviet UN embassy early in 1968, Malik attacked Israel as an aggressor and said to Goldberg something to the effect of, "You Americans don't know what it's like to have your country occupied but we Russians do, and that's why we have so much compassion for occupied peoples." To which Goldberg replied, "You Russians are quite expert and have a pretty good reputation for occupying other peoples' countries, so don't give me that kind of boiler-plate." While this occurred at a private meeting, Goldberg also responded sharply on other occasions at open UN meetings.

10. David Easton, *A Framework for Political Analysis* (Englewood

Cliffs, N.J.: Prentice-Hall, 1965), p. 132. Easton defines a "disturbance" as referring to activities in the environment or within a system "that can be expected to or do displace a system from its current pattern of operations, regardless of whether or not it is stressful for the system" (p. 91). Disturbances vary with the consequences and are classified as neutral, benign, or stressful. Some disturbances threaten to prevent the system from functioning and therefore can be called stressful, but a disturbance can stress a system without destroying it.

12/ Congress and USUN

The precedent set by President Eisenhower in this matter and continued by this [Kennedy] Administration, seems unfortunate. The Ambassador to the United Nations is not a second Secretary of State, but the present arrangement suggests a certain imbalance in the role assigned to the UN delegation in the policy-making process. . . . The UN delegation in New York should not operate a second foreign office. Such confusion of responsibility reinforces a tendency to give undue weight in national foreign policy formulation to considerations that seem more important in New York than they seem in Washington, D.C.

This statement is contained in a speech by Senator Henry M. Jackson (D., Wash.) made March 20, 1962, before the National Press Club.[1] It was an address replete with doubts as to the usefulness of the UN to "our vital interests." He asserted that "the conduct of UN affairs absorbs a disproportionate amount of energy of our highest officials," that there was too much voting on too many issues in the UN. His focus of criticism, however, was the USUN:

> *I have been struck, for example, by the serious disproportion in the press, radio and television coverage of our UN delegation and the coverage of the Department of State. The space and time devoted to the former does not correctly reflect the relative importance of what is said in New York against what is said in Washington. . . .*
>
> *Should our delegation in the United Nations play a larger role in the policy-making process than our representatives to NATO or to major world capitals? I think the answer is no and the burden of proof should lie upon those who advocate a unique role for our Embassy in New York.*[2]

What makes Senator Jackson's words particularly cogent is that they represent part of a continuing but low-key debate in Congress as to how the Mission should function; indeed, how it *does* function. For example, in the Hickenlooper-Mansfield report occurs the following assessment:

> *It is certainly the case that the official position on almost any issue is spelled out by Washington in very minute detail. The delegation is guided very closely not only on questions of substance but even on matters of procedure.*

The two Senators found this a highly inefficient procedure:

Nevertheless, during the course of a General Assembly, unanticipated developments often create a need for changes— frequently minor changes—in positions or procedure. These changes almost invariably require prior clearance from Washington. The requirement would not be so burdensome, perhaps, if only one bureau of the Department of State were involved in sanctioning them. Not infrequently, however, even a slight change in the phrase of a statement of an official position at the UN may call for clearance by any number of bureaus and offices scattered throughout various executive agencies and departments.[3]

The Senators hesitated to suggest where precisely "the line ought to be drawn between firm central control over policy and flexibility in its pursuit at the United Nations."

Similar criticism was voiced by Hamilton Fish Armstrong a few years later.[4] He reported that occasionally the USUN has been reproved for failing to consult with allies and neutrals. Defending the delegation, Armstrong writes:

Often the fault has been in the White House or the State Department, where decisions were delayed and instructions withheld till the 11th hour. The delegation then had no time to explain the American position at length and the requests for support which it hastily sent out were so urgent that they sounded peremptory and as though they took the recipient's vote for granted. This is not leadership.

It is to be noted that large sections of the Hickenlooper-Mansfield report are quoted in Ambassador Pedersen's article without comment.[5] In selecting these passages from the Senate document, it may be assumed that he approves of what may be regarded as a reprimand of State Department procedures.

The heart of the dispute, however, is untouched by this part of the debate. The concern that the USUN should remain subordinate to the State Department can no longer (if, indeed, it ever could) be easily solved. As Carl J. Friedrich has suggested:

> *The starting point of any study of responsibility must be that even under the best arrangements a considerable margin of irresponsible conduct of administrative activities is inevitable.*[6]

How would Senator Jackson propose to cut the USUN down to its proper size? A tougher I.O. Bureau? Nobody was tougher, so far as I can judge, than Harlan Cleveland as Assistant Secretary for I.O. Affairs, nor was his deputy, Richard N. Gardner, any easier to get along with. Yet when Adlai Stevenson decided to change United States policy on Article 19 of the UN Charter, he changed it and hard-nosed New Frontiersmen like Cleveland and Gardner could not do a thing about it and did not even try. One observer-participant told me that the Washington policy-makers are at the mercy of the Mission staff:

> *The worst thing about this Mission is those people here who still carry on the 'winking' tradition. They will, for example, state the United States line to the Africans or the Russians; then comes the wink—don't worry, we'll negotiate.*

So long as there is a strong political incentive for a President to go outside the Foreign Service for the USUN Chief and for delegates to the General Assembly, the kind of tidy discipline which any bureaucracy aspires to for the sake of coherence and its own self-extension will be quite unattainable. The "winking" tradition will go uncorrected and unpunished so long as the USUN Chief not only allows it to go on but also does a bit of winking himself. In short, having accepted public diplomacy as an integral part of American policy-making, as Britain in the seventeenth century accepted public government,[7] the USUN Chief and his ad interim delegates must be public men with public lives and public responsibilities or, more precisely, with responsibilities to varied publics. This may not always be the case, as when a President appoints a famous movie star or concert singer. It is questionable whether American foreign policy benefited greatly from the occasional epiphany at the UN of Irene Dunne.[8]

An additional complicating factor is whether or not a USUN Chief becomes more valuable as his length of service increases—more valuable, that is, to the effectuation of American foreign policy. Of course, the longer he stays, it may be argued, the greater his influence and the more difficult it is to superintend his activities at the UN. The British view has been expressed privately by Lord Caradon, United Kingdom Mission Chief, who is said to be against long service at the UN because of the danger of "UNization" (pronounced "you-enization").

For the UN, there is no doubt that a Mission Chief's length of service raises his status in the UN subsystem, just as seniority does in many other subsystems. Dag Hammarskjöld once wrote that the establishment of UN permanent delegations was a contribution to diplomacy which "may well come to be regarded as the most important 'common law' development which has taken place so far within the constitutional framework of the Charter."[9] In an address in 1959, he went into even greater detail as to the meaning of the permanent missions to the UN:

> *Over the years, the diplomatic representatives accredited to the United Nations have developed a cooperation and built mutual contacts in dealing with problems they have in common, which in reality make them members of a kind of continuous diplomatic conference, in which they are informally following and able to discuss, on a personal basis, all political questions which are important for the work of the Organization. . . . Public debate in the United Nations is dominated by the same differences among the parties as international political life as a whole. But behind closed doors these differences are diluted. The human factor carries more weight there, and confidential exchanges are possible even across frontiers which otherwise appear impassable.*[10]

The presence at each session of the General Assembly of two congressmen has given the USUN additional resources and has affected congressional understanding of what the UN is doing.[11] The educational effect of the arrangement is of some value, as can be noted from examining their reports made annually to Congress upon completion of their UN assignment.

In 1947, Senators Vandenberg and Tom Connally were appointed as delegates to the General Assembly. They were the first. Then came a hiatus until 1950. Senator Vandenberg questioned whether a congressman acting as a UN delegate would be serving two masters—Congress, of which he was a member, and the President, whose instructions he was bound to follow. He wrote in a letter to Eleanor Roosevelt that he was "increasingly impressed with the difficulties confronted by 'Congressional' representatives because of their dual capacity."[12] Senator Vandenberg's apprehensions no longer seem to weigh heavily upon Congress. After all, the chairmen and ranking representatives of the Foreign Affairs committees of both Houses and of both parties had been involved during World War II and thereafter in various aspects of foreign policy so that the noun "bipartisanship" (or "nonpartisanship") had some reality, although its real meaning to foreign policy has been blurred by its virtuous-sounding echoes.[13]

From 1948 to 1950, there was no congressional delegation to the annual General Assembly session. The custom was revived when a consensus arose over the need for Executive-congressional cooperation, if not on all foreign policy issues, then certainly at the UN itself. Two senators or two representatives are appointed annually, the understanding being that one of the two is to be a Republican and the other a Democrat. The senators are appointed in election years and the representatives in off years.[14] Upon resumption of the custom, the first pair to be appointed were Senator Henry Cabot Lodge and Senator John Sparkman. Since then, there have been influential senators like Green, Humphrey,[15] Knowland, Mansfield, Morse, Pastore, Alexander Smith, and Wiley. With a Congress sympathetic to USUN as an institution, a President who will probably always want at the UN his own rather than the State Department's man, and the willingness of elite Americans to serve as USUN Chief or in subordinate delegate posts, USUN influence will continue to grow to such an extent that no State Department policy either of rollback or containment of USUN will work. At best, the State Department can accept, as it has, a policy of competitive coexistence with USUN.

Notes

1. *Congressional Record*, March 21, 1962, pp. 4277–4278. This kind of criticism in Congress was not confined to the USUN Chief. In the *Vandenberg Papers* we read that Senator Vandenberg issued a statement criticizing Henry A. Wallace's Madison Square Garden speech September 12, 1946, in which Vandenberg said that most Republicans were for a bipartisan foreign policy, "but the situation equally requires unity within the Administration itself. We can only cooperate with one Secretary of State at a time." (*The Private Papers of Arthur H. Vandenberg, Jr.* [New York: Houghton Mifflin, 1952], p. 300.)
2. *Congressional Record, op. cit.*

3. U.S. Senate, "Observations on the United Nations," *Sen. Doc. 26*, 86th Cong., 1st Sess., 1959, pp. 6–7.

4. Hamilton Fish Armstrong, "The UN On Trial," *Foreign Affairs*, XXXIX, No. 3 (April 1961), 386–415.

5. Richard F. Pedersen, "National Representation in the United Nations," *International Organization*, XV, No. 2 (Spring 1961), 258.

6. In Peter Woll (ed.), *Public Administration and Policy* (New York: Harper and Row Torchbooks, 1966), p. 222. President Kennedy reacted unconcernedly to the Jackson criticism. At his news conference March 21, 1962, a day after Senator Jackson's speech, the President quite tactfully disagreed with the Senator. "I support the United Nations very strongly," said the President, "and I think the American people do—not because its power is unlimited and not because we commit our policy to the United Nations so much as because we believe that it serves the interests of the United States, and the interests of the United States are in an association of free people working together to maintain the peace."

7. Introduction, John Plamenatz (ed.), *Readings from Liberal Writers* (New York: Barnes and Noble, 1965), p. 23: "The claim was now made, as never before, that government should be conducted in public in the presence of the people's representatives. There was now, as there used not to be, something which men were soon to call *public opinion*—meaning by it, not the customs and beliefs which in all countries, even the most primitive or despotically governed, limit power, but the critical attitude to government of a mass of persons who follow its day-to-day activities."

8. Armstrong, *op. cit.*: "Race, color, religion, sex and party do not by themselves, constitute qualifications for helping the Permanent Representative and his associates negotiate on some of the most difficult and important problems of the world." Conor Cruise O'Brien tells the story that in September 1957, Miss Dunne, a Catholic, was given a "theo-political" assignment by Ambassador Lodge. She carried the message to Cardinal Spellman that the Irish delegation would vote "Yes" instead of "No" on the upcoming UN discussion on the representation of China question. The Cardinal then pressed Frank Aiken, the Foreign Minister, to reverse the delegation vote, but Aiken declined. (Conor Cruise O'Brien, *To Katanga and Back: A UN Case History* [New York: Simon and Schuster, 1963], p. 23.)

9. Wilder Foote (ed.), *Dag Hammarskjold: Servant of Peace. A Selection of His Speeches and Statements* (New York: Harper and Row, 1962), p. 224.

10. *Ibid.*, p. 201. Harold Lasswell quotes from Charles K. Webster, *The Foreign Policy of Castlereagh:* "The sovereigns and statesmen of the different countries had lived a common life for almost two years. They had shared trials and triumphs and even board and lodging for long periods together. Those who had experienced the emotions produced by the final overthrow of Napoleon never completely lost a peculiar intimacy. . . . With all their jealousies and intrigues they had been, as it were, comrades for a considerable period." (Harold Lasswell, *World Politics and Personal Insecurity* [New York: Macmillan paperback, 1965], p. 180.) Also see Charles Winchmore, "The Secretariat: Retrospect and Prospect," in N. J. Padelford and L. M. Goorich (eds.), *The United Nations in the Balance: Accomplishments and Prospects* (New York: Praeger, 1965), p. 271.

11. James A. Robinson, *Congress and Foreign Policy-Making* (Homewood, Ill.: Dorsey, 1962), p. 198: "Perhaps the most dramatic effect of a change in attitude as a result of this kind of experience [serving as a UN delegate] is the case of Rep. Walter Judd (R., Minnesota) who after his service at the United Nations in 1957 changed his position about the United Nations Technical Assistance program. There have also been instances in which Congressional members of the delegation influence U.S. policy at the United Nations. In 1957, for example, Rep. A. S. J. Carnahan (D., Missouri), assigned to the Fifth Committee, successfully managed U.S. efforts to alter the system for raising money for the U.N. budget. When assigned to this committee he was asked to lay the groundwork for the United States to push for a change in the budget allotment procedures in a later year and not to expect to succeed that time. However, largely through his own form of quiet diplomacy the result was achieved in that very session."

12. Vandenberg, *op. cit.*, p. 331: "Of course it will always be true that a man cannot serve two masters. Yet that is precisely what I undertake to do—for example when I, as a Senator, sit in the General Assembly as a delegate, I am helping to make decisions for the United Nations which must pass in review before the American Congress. Having participated in the United Nations in helping to make the decisions, I am not a 'free agent' when I return to the Senate to function in my 'Congressional' capacity. Indeed, it could be a most embarrassing and difficult situation in the event that I did not approve of some decision made by the United Nations. I should dislike to oppose in Congress anything to which I had given my consent (if only by reluctant acquiescence) in the United Nations."

[Vandenberg pointed out to Mrs. Roosevelt that UN delegates were

13/ State Department and USUN: Who, Whom?

What makes life easier for USUN and its Chief and contributes to their influence-breeding charisma is that the State Department is fair game for encroachments by almost anybody with some power, influence, or constituency.[1] Since the State Department is visibly involved in rough, amoral power politics, it is the Department and its Secretary who bear the burdens of what ill will may arise among some publics and pressure groups. The USUN, meanwhile, being involved in the "nonpower politics" environment of the UN—if only by definition—can at worst be accused of being ineffectual. When a television audience watches the American spokesman at the Security Council, it is not seeing "expediency" in not "free agents," that by the very commissions which they held they rightfully voted as instructed by the President, and with possibly a subsequent moral obligation to defend this position in Congress. The question, Vandenberg surmised, went to the heart of the traditiona "checks and balances" of American governmental system. At the sam time he urged continuity in American representation at the Gene Assembly. Vandenberg suggested to Mrs. Roosevelt that delegates to Assembly perhaps should hold full-time, year-around jobs in order the nation be "adequately prepared" for Assembly work.] (Letter January 9, 1947.)

13. James MacGregor Burns, "Excellence in President and Con in Stephen Graubard and Gerald Holton (eds.), *Excellence and ship in a Democracy* (New York: Columbia University Press, 1 170, note 19: "The virtues of bipartisanship are uncritically acc this country because it has come to stand for cooperation bet two presidential parties. But bipartisanship, in a four-party also cooperation between the two congressional parties. . . . advocates of bipartisanship really support, of course, is not anism itself but the liberal internationalist policies that they it." Robert Dahl has written: "Bipartisanship testifies to th of a party system to reflect accurately the unities and diver a nation. For what bipartisanship in Congress reflects is t nation may be divided on domestic issues and at the sam a national majority on foreign policy, cutting athwart th alignments of domestic policy." (*Congress and Forei* York: Norton, 1964], p. 232.)

14. Channing B. Richardson, "U.S. Mission to t *tional Organization*, VII, No. 1 (February 1953), 23

15. As an example of how even powerful senators foreign policy, the following may be of interest: A November 1956 Hungarian crisis, Miss Anna Kethl in the beleaguered Imre Nagy government, had h her country before the UN. She received the c United States delegation. One afternoon she wa Humphrey during a visit to the UN Delegate whether she had met "Cabot," meaning Aml had not. A friend of hers said that the Unite clined to see her. Humphrey's face clouded, to wait and he would bring "Cabot" back. H effort by Senator Knowland was unsuccessf

200

action, but rather moral leadership, ideology, the rhetoric of fair play. The UN and therefore USUN afford an outlet for the satisfaction of normative standards which seem to conflict directly with the State Department. At the UN, the audience can see open diplomacy, the personal touch, the direct approach, the rational and simple answer, the parry-and-thrust debate, while the State Department lies hidden, silent, unapproachable.

Popular tradition, practitioners of which are sometimes Presidents seeking a scapegoat, blames the State Department for the nation's foreign policy troubles. Once it was "cookie-pushers in Foggy Bottom," then Fascists (for "selling out" Republican Spain or making deals with Admiral Darlan), or "Communist spies," or, presently, "warmongers." President Roosevelt once told Marriner S. Eccles:

You should go through the experience of trying to get any changes in the thinking, policy and action of the career diplomats and then you'd know what a real problem was.[2]

President Kennedy, apparently, felt even less confidence in the State Department, according to Theodore Sorenson, who writes:

The President was discouraged with the State Department almost as soon as he took office. He felt that it too often seemed to have a built-in inertia which deadened initiative and that its tendency toward excessive delay obscured determination.[3]

The "Other" State Department

Joseph Kraft has quoted Dean Acheson as saying, "Nobody has been able to run the [State] Department in 150 years."[4] It is even fashionable for the Secretary of State (particularly when he is before a congressional committee) to demonstrate that he is as aware of his department's weaknesses as any congressman.[5] Joseph McCarthy in his heyday managed to move in on the State Department, whether it had to do with ambassadorial appointments or foreign policy.[6]

In 1962, twenty-six persons or agencies were consistently involved in foreign affairs, twelve in the Executive Office of the President and fourteen outside: Defense, Treasury, Justice, State, Agriculture, Commerce, Labor, AEC, NASA, USIA, Export-Import Bank, Tariff Commission, and Foreign Claims Settlements Commission.[7] One reason why the State Department is a nice, fat target is that by its nature it cannot speak as candidly to the press as can other government officials with no direct responsibility to the foreign policy process. James Reston has written:

What influence the press has on the conduct of foreign policy often comes indirectly, not through the mass of the people, but mainly through the Congress of the United States. . . . So the reporter and the Congressman are often natural allies.[8]

The encroachment on State Department policy preserves is age-old and apparently doomed to go on for a long time. Usually, however, the trespass has been by outside agencies—J. Edgar Hoover and the FBI,[9] or the Assistant Secretary of Defense for International Security Affairs, or others. In the USUN, we see the phenomenon of an embassy, an agency, a bureau, a division—whatever it may be on the chart—within the State Department which has little direct supervision to worry about except from the President himself.[10] The organization chart of *le pays légal* shows a rigid hierarchical structure. A wheel chart based on *le pays réel* might be more correct, if not overimaginative. Yet can a viewer of international organization be accused of hyperimagination when we deal with a USUN which, while possessing no more legal power than that of representing the President at the UN, has *power*—and with a UN which has fully stated legal powers, yet has no power to coerce anybody, including the Maldive Islands or Yemen?[11] One reason for USUN power, and certainly influence, is its open existence in a fairly open society: the UN. The State Department, necessarily involved in the politics of expediency, must consider its various audiences—the American publics, our allies, the Third World, the Communist bloc, the UN— when it looks at its "worry list" of world problems and when it sets up its priorities. It is then that one sees that State Department priorities are not the same as USUN priorities. Southwest Africa may be a big rhetorical or political issue in the UN, where the overwhelming majority of countries are ex-colonial, non-white, and poor. Southwest Africa has none of this urgency to a State

Department which represents one of two nuclear super-powers. The USUN has to worry about UN "peace-keeping" operations with a far greater fervor than need the State Department.

Priorities for any embassy are fixed by (*a*) the host country's domestic and foreign policies and (*b*) the State Department and United States foreign policy. This cannot be true for the USUN because it inhabits several sub-systems whose boundaries float free and sometimes disappear. That is why the chart I have prepared to describe the USUN represents a radical deviation from the customary extraterrestrial view of the Mission. Perhaps the chart may be exaggerated, but it may in time seem understated. Surely, there is no reason why in a country where foreign policy-making is polyarchical and where dissonances, official and unofficial, on foreign policy are virtually endemic, a USUN Chief cannot create his own cosmos, his own foreign policy mechanism for doing what comes naturally.

After all, it was Secretary Rusk who once said:

There are those who think that the heart of a bureaucracy is a struggle for power. This is not the case at all. The heart of the bureaucratic problem is the inclination to avoid responsibility. One of the reasons that organization seldom gets in the way of a good man is that if a man demonstrates that he is willing to make judgments and decisions and live with the results, power gravitates to him because other people will get out of his way.[12]

If it all happened in the manner Rusk describes, political scientists would save a lot of time they devote to systems analysis.[13] It is not, however, quite that way in the State Department living system, even for the "good man" willing to make judgments and decisions. The word "decision" has specific meaning:

A *decision is a policy involving severe sanctions (deprivations). . . . Power is participation in the making of decisions. . . . It is the threat of sanctions which differentiates power from influence in general. Power is a special case of the exercise of influence; it is the process of affecting policies of others with the help of (actual or threatened) severe deprivations for non-conformity with the policies intended.*[14]

Since I have argued that USUN and its Chief have influence and power bordering on autonomy, a question arises from the Lasswell-Kaplan abstraction. There are no visible sanctions which USUN can impose on anybody; it is as powerless in this respect as any other embassy. The USUN Chief could resign with a blast against United States foreign policy, but it has not happened yet. One could therefore say that USUN and its head have little power since they can impose no sanctions. On the other hand, what sanctions can the State Department impose on a USUN Chief? Not many, as we noted in the case of Adlai Stevenson.[15] However, the UN, in a parliamentary sense, can impose sanctions on its members. I do not refer to extraordinary deprivations, such as creating economic instability (which it cannot, as in the cases of

South Africa and Rhodesia) or military insecurity, but rather to victory or defeat on resolutions where propaganda victories are important. Since the United States accepts the UN as a forum where there is some kind of decision-making going on, the UN can impose sanctions in the nature of weakening (negative sanctions) or strengthening (positive) United States influence. Thus, one may argue that what weakens USUN or the USUN Chief weakens that sector of United States foreign policy which interacts with UN policies. It may also be argued that when the USUN Chief enjoys the President's confidence (as Stevenson did not, but Goldberg did), United States policies are strengthened at the UN.

Sanction theory as a facet in the study of power is difficult, if not confusing, in the USUN-State relationship, since both may be weak in sanction-imposition prerogatives. However, it is possible that if the President wants the USUN Chief to remain influential—in other words, if he has a temporary indispensability to the sovereign—this resource of the USUN Chief becomes a potential sanction against the Department of State.

If neither State nor USUN possessed decisive coercive power one over the other, then we could argue that they had reached some kind of "you can't win 'em all" equilibrium. This would be true, however, if and only if there were no third subsystem, the UN, to upset equilibrium. What, then, can we say about the State Department and the "other" State Department? We could say about

USUN, in the Aristotelian spirit, that a thing is either A or non-A. Either USUN is a subordinate embassy or it is not; either it belongs to the State Department or to the UN; either the USUN Chief is an ambassador or he is not. It will be obvious that Aristotle's categories severely cramp a definition of USUN in the same way that a Hobbesian choice—either absolute power or total anarchy —is too rigorous.

Perhaps in dealing with USUN we ought to adopt the Heraclitus maxim: "It is and it is not." Heraclitus may well have the answer to the questions raised in this study, not only in its specific concern but in regard to political science generally.

Notes

1. "The State Department has virtually no 'constituency.' It is not the kind of service agency whose benefits are immediately visible to important voting blocs; therefore, it cannot easily mobilize citizen pressures on Congress. . . . The State Department, moreover, is a small department; its personnel is recruited almost wholly on a career basis; it has little patronage to dispense. . . . There are other, more irrational factors, on the debit side of the Department's balance sheet." Robert A. Dahl, *Congress and Foreign Policy* (New York: Norton, 1964), pp. 112–113.

2. Richard E. Neustadt, *Presidential Power, The Politics of Leadership* (New York: John Wiley, 1960), p. 42.

3. Theodore Sorenson, *Kennedy* (New York: Bantam, 1966), p. 322.

4. In *Harper's Magazine* (November 1961), cited in James McCamy, *Conduct of the New Diplomacy* (New York: Harper and Row, 1964), p. 7.

5. See in Henry M. Jackson (ed.), *The Secretary of State and the*

Ambassador (New York: Praeger, 1964), p. 125, Dean Rusk's statement: "When I read a telegram coming in in the morning, it poses a very specific question, and the moment I read it I know myself what the answer must be. But that telegram goes on its appointed courses into the bureau, and through the office and down to the desk. If it doesn't go down there, somebody feels that he is being deprived of his participation in a matter of his responsibility.

"Then it goes from the action officer back up through the Department to me a week or ten days later, and if it isn't the answer that I knew had to be the answer, then I change it at that point, having taken into account the advice that came from below. But usually it is the answer that everybody would know has to be the answer."

6. Richard H. Rovere, *Senator Joe McCarthy* (Cleveland: World, 1960), pp. 4 *et passim.*

7. McCamy, *op. cit.*, p. 35. I have omitted the American Battle Monuments Commission, which also gets into the act, somehow.

8. James Reston, "The Press and Foreign Policy," *Foreign Affairs*, XLIV, No. 4 (July 1966), 566.

9. "Rusk Hints Hoover Assents on Consuls," read the headline on a Washington story in *The New York Times*, January 21, 1967. The report discussed the proposed consular treaty with the Soviet Union to permit mutual increase in the number of consulates in both countries. The Senate had been delaying ratification of the treaty because of a Hoover statement that the Russians would find greater espionage opportunities with an increase in consulates. Secretary Rusk wrote the FBI Director a letter asking him to amplify his views before the House Appropriations Committee. Hoover's reply was short, cryptic, and not regarded as helpful. President Johnson some weeks later had to address himself to the problem at a press conference during which he announced Hoover's approval of the treaty. The FBI's domain could well be examined from the standpoint of unusual autonomy, not merely within a single department but within the entire federal government.

10. The supervision may have its lighter moments, as may be seen in this extract from a speech by Ambassador Goldberg: "Another fact . . . is that in all this oratorical effort I have had the advantage of a great amount of coaching from the sidelines. One of my first TV fan messages, which was brought to me in the Security Council during the Kashmir crisis nearly two years ago, said, 'Arthur, don't look down so—keep your head up.' That was from President Johnson." (*USUN Press Release* 127, July 27, 1967, p. 1.)

11. The concept of "power" is crucial in this context, yet difficult to

quantify. "Power cannot be counted exactly," writes Karl Deutsch, "but it can be estimated in proportion to the power resources or capabilities that are visibly available, such as the numbers of countable supporters, voters, or soldiers available or required in a particular political context." (*The Nerves of Government* [New York: Free Press, paperback, 1966], p. 120.) The USUN Chief has no military divisions, but obviously has supporters. The estimated five thousand pieces of mail and editorials favorable to Adlai Stevenson which flooded USUN headquarters during the October 1962 Cuba crisis (see, above, Chapter 9, note 10) so affected the White House that a high Washington official at the time telephoned Clayton Fritchey in New York and, reportedly, said: "Okay, you win, stop." Fritchey stopped.

12. Jackson, *op. cit.*, p. 124.

13. "Systems analysis is concerned with the building of models that abstract from reality but represent the crucial relationships one is interested in studying. The systems analyst first decides what questions are relevant to his inquiry, selects certain quantifiable factors . . . and then gives them quantitative relationships with one another within the system he has chosen for analysis." (Aaron Wildavsky, "The Political Economy of Efficiency," *The Public Interest*, No. 8 [Summer 1967], p. 34.)

14. Harold D. Lasswell and Abraham Kaplan, *Power and Society* (New Haven: Yale University Press, 1950), quoted in Robert A. Dahl, *Modern Political Analysis* (Englewood Cliffs, N.J.: Prentice-Hall, 1963), p. 51.

15. In spring 1966, there were reports circulating that Justice Goldberg and the State Department were not getting along well at all. For example, it was noted that he was not listed as a speaker at the season's State Department briefing for the news media, nor as it turned out had he been invited to be a speaker. This was rather unusual since the USUN Chief normally is an important figure at these off-the-record briefings where the Administration tries to sell its policies. When a close friend of Goldberg was asked about this singular omission—depriving the USUN Chief of a useful platform—the friend replied, "Goldberg will do his own briefing that week. He's speaking at the National Press Club." I know that the Ambassador was irritated at the omission "sanction."

CHART 1

Organization Chart of the Permanent United States Mission to the United Nations

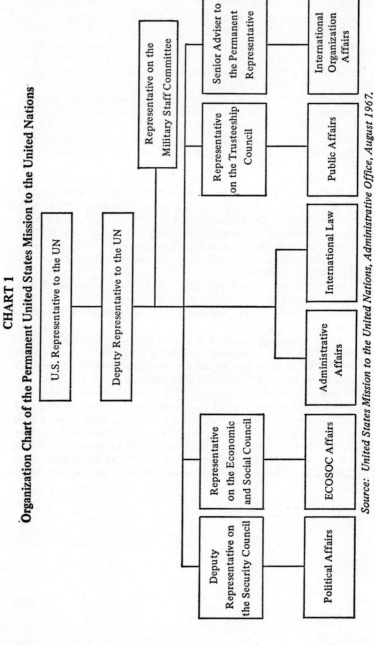

Source: *United States Mission to the United Nations, Administrative Office, August 1967.*

CHART 2

Organization Chart of a United States Delegation to a United Nations General Assembly Session

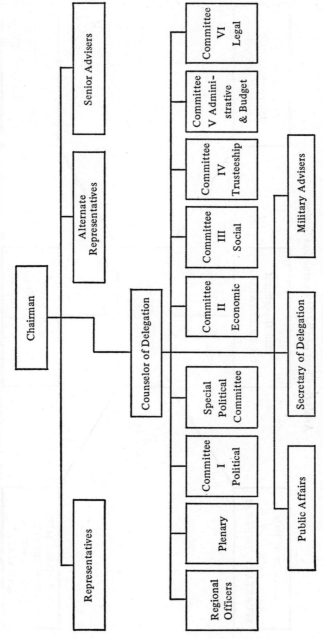

Source: United States Mission to the United Nations, Administrative Office, December 1965.

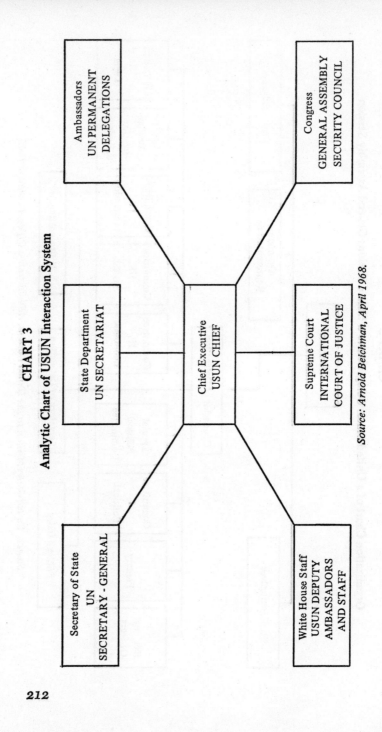

CHART 3

Analytic Chart of USUN Interaction System

Ambassadors UN PERMANENT DELEGATIONS	
State Department UN SECRETARIAT	Secretary of State UN SECRETARY - GENERAL
Chief Executive USUN CHIEF	
Supreme Court INTERNATIONAL COURT OF JUSTICE	White House Staff USUN DEPUTY AMBASSADORS AND STAFF
Congress GENERAL ASSEMBLY SECURITY COUNCIL	

Source: Arnold Beichman, April 1968.

Name Index

Name Index

Name Index

Subject Index

Subject Index

Subject Index

Third World, 31, 203
Trusteeship Council, UN, 74, 76

UN (United Nations): autonomy
loss in, 54; bilateral diplomacy
of, 55–56; Conference on Trade
and Development, 131; Congress and, 39; as cornerstone
of foreign policy, 21; elaborate
U.S. representation in, 59; first
Secretary-General, 20; host
country responsibilities, 76;
headquarters in U.S., 20, 40–
41; Headquarters Agreement,
40; ideological foundation of,
60–61; "influence" in, 62; influence of speech in, 73–74; interdepartmental committees in,
90–92; living system of, 61;
multilateral diplomacy and, 46–
65; and permanent missions,
viii–xii; policy-making in, 60;
privileges and immunities of,
41–42; public support of,
22; Secretariat Building, 72;
statutory basis for U.S. participation in, 37–38; subsystems in, 184; in Suez crisis, 25–
26; "uniqueness" of, 28; U.S.
commitment to, 114; U.S. foreign policy and, 19–31, 38–39;
U.S. influence on policy of,
118; U.S. strategy in, 30; U.S.
support for, 20–22; USUN
strength and, 10; value to U.S.,
24; veto power over U.S. foreign policy, 27; voting and roll-
call procedure in, 51–52; world
crises and, 26–29; see also
United Nations (adj.)
"UNationizing" (UNization), 136,
193
UN Charter: Article 19 of, 149;
authorization in, 40; as compromise, 50; headquarters location and, 41; as ideological
foundation, 60–61

United Nations, see UN
United Nations Economic Com-
mittee, 91
United Nations Emergency Force,
112, 150
Universal Declaration of Human
Rights, 98
United States: "elaborate" representation of in UN, 59; end
of nuclear monopoly by, 31;
foreign policy as affected by
UN, 19–31, 119; loss of automatic majority in UN, 30, 118;
policy-making and executive
structure in UN, 23–24, 60;
Senate Foreign Relations Committee, 128; and South Africa,
169
United States Mission to the
United Nations, see USUN
U.S.S.R., see Soviet Union
USUN (United States Mission to
the United Nations): alliances
with publics, 10; ambassador to,
see Chief of Mission; appropriations for, 77; autonomy of,
10, 107–108; bargaining power
of, 118; "boundary" of within
State Department, 7–8; chief
representative in, 4–5 (see also
Chief of Mission); Congress
and, 113, 189–196; Constitution and, 6; corporate personality of, 72; dual role in, 4–6;
dysfunctional role of, 11–12;
early days of, 177–186; foreign
policy and, 19–31, 38–39, 119;
as foreign policy subsystem, xv;
as "foreign power," 13; functioning of, 72–82; hierarchical
ties in, 95; home rule prerogatives of, xv; increased bargaining
power of, 113; information-
gathering by, 74; institutionalized nature of, 47, 131–132;
and International Organization
Bureau, 90–96, 117–118; and

220